Making Clothes for Your Dog

How to Sew and Knit Outfits that Keep Your Dog Warm and Looking Great

Making Clothes for Your Dog

How to Sew and Knit Outfits that Keep Your Dog Warm and Looking Great

Design Originals

an Imprint of Fox Chapel Publishing

www.d-originals.com

Credits for the English Edition
Acquisition editor: **Peg Couch**
Copy editor: **Katie Weeber**
Cover and layout designer: **Ashley Millhouse**
Editor: **Colleen Dorsey**
Technical editor: **Choly Knight**

팅크따라 강아지 옷 만들기 : 우리 강아지를 위한 귀엽고 사랑스러운 옷&소품
by JISU LEE (이지수)
Copyright © 2010 Sigongsa Co., Ltd.
All rights reserved.
Originally published in Korea by Sigongsa Co., Ltd.
English translation copyright © 2013 New Design Originals Corporation
Arranged with Sigongsa Co., Ltd through LEE's Literary Agency, Taiwan

ISBN 978-1-57421-610-3

Making Clothes for Your Dog is an abridged translation of the original Korean language book. This version published by New Design Originals Corporation, an imprint of Fox Chapel Publishing Company, Inc., East Petersburg, PA.

Library of Congress Cataloging-in-Publication Data

Lee, Jisu.
    [T'ingk'u ttara kangaji ot mandulgi. English]
    Making clothes for your dog / Jisu Lee.
        pages cm
    Includes index.
    ISBN 978-1-57421-610-3
    1. Dogs--Equipment and supplies. 2. Sewing. 3. Costume. I. Title.
    SF427.15.L44 2013
    646.4'78--dc23
                        2013029023

Printed in China
First printing

Preface

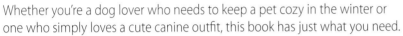

Whether you're a dog lover who needs to keep a pet cozy in the winter or one who simply loves a cute canine outfit, this book has just what you need.

Korean sewing aficionado and pet blogger Tingk (Jisu Lee) has spent years making clothes for dogs of all shapes, sizes, and breeds. This volume compiles an adorable array of her designs for dog clothing both practical and endearing: shirts, dresses, capes, bathrobes, aprons, a bridal gown and tuxedo, and even traditional Korean dress, "hanbok." You're sure to be charmed, just as we were, by the diverse designs, the amazing fabrics, and the enthusiastic canine companions who model it all. With straightforward patterns and detailed instructions, you'll be making stylish duds for your dogs in no time. And look for a second volume by Tingk in late 2014, which will feature a variety of doggie accessories like hats, bags, toys, and bedding.

Tingk joins the rapidly growing collection of talented craft authors from around the world selected for inclusion in the Design Originals line. Known for its innovative topics and highly regarded authors, Design Originals will continue to bring the best selections of foreign and American craft books to North American readers. We love these books, and we hope you will, too. Enjoy!

Carole

Carole Giagnocavo
Publisher
carole@d-originals.com

About the Author

The author's dogs, Furryhead and Gucci.

Jisu Lee (known as Tingk)

Years ago, Tingk worked at an editorial design company, but left her job after she got married. During the first year of her marriage, she adopted her first pets, Jjanga (Furryhead) and Gujji (Gucci), and she started learning handicrafts. Today, Furryhead and Gucci are old dogs, 10 years old.

When Tingk adopted her dogs, raising pets wasn't very popular, so it was difficult to get quality food, clothing, and so on for dogs. She also wasn't so sure whether mass-produced items for dogs were safe or not. Dogs have very delicate, sensitive skin, and Tingk wanted to make comfortable, pretty clothes with soft, nice fabrics for her dogs. So she started making clothes for canines and got more and more

involved in the world of crafts. She took several craft courses on clothing, Korean traditional clothing (Hanbok), and accessories. Tingk also applies her skills in quilting, felting, and other crafts to make clothes for dogs.

Now Tingk also has two cats, Hope (a 4-year-old) and Shabel (a 2-year-old). She makes not only dog clothes but cat clothes and items, too. She's having a great time making pet clothes, and she posts fun entries with her dogs and cats on her blog and on Facebook. Check her out here:
tingkstyle.com
facebook.com/tingkstyle

Introduction: Making One-of-a-Kind Adorable Clothes for Your Dogs!

In the year I got married, our dogs Furryhead and Gucci joined our family and started to bond deeply with us. Seeing them growing up day by day, I had the desire to make them some clothes on my own. In the beginning I was all thumbs and made lousy products. I felt totally satisfied, however, when I saw Furryhead and Gucci putting on my handmade clothes and happily playing around. Time flies—Furryhead and Gucci have been with us for ten years now. My pet-clothes-making skills are also getting better and better.

Many people might think it is good enough to buy their dogs' clothes and accessories in animal hospitals or pet stores. However, each dog is unique and might not fit in mass-produced clothing. Nowadays, more and more people are aware of this fact and willingly take out their sewing kits to make pet clothes on their own. In order to help these people, in this book I have shared all my experiences and methodologies for making pet clothes as much as possible. The method for making pet clothes is very similar to that for making human clothes. The biggest difference is that the body shape of pets is very different from that of human beings. Therefore you need to understand the body formation and characteristics of your pets before making pet clothes for them. In the beginning, you might encounter some setbacks. Don't worry. Just keep going with love and care for your pets. I believe you can make very unique and lovely pet clothes for your pets!

I would like to thank many people for helping me along the way with this book. First off, I would like to thank my family for their continuous support. I also want to express my sincere gratitude to all the staff, sewing masters, cute dog models, and their owners who contributed their efforts and made this book possible. My special thanks go to Sigongsa Co. Ltd., Miss Ji Yoon, the photographers, and the art designers who made this book such a beautiful publication. Of course, I won't forget those online friends who cheer me up on my blogs. Thank you all!

Last but not least, I hope this book can become a stepping-stone for you to learn sewing. For those readers who think it is very difficult to sew pet clothes, I hope you can challenge yourself with confidence after reading this book!

Tingk

Contents

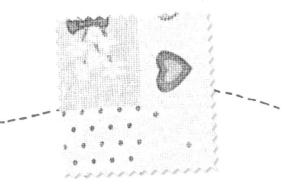

Part I

Projects

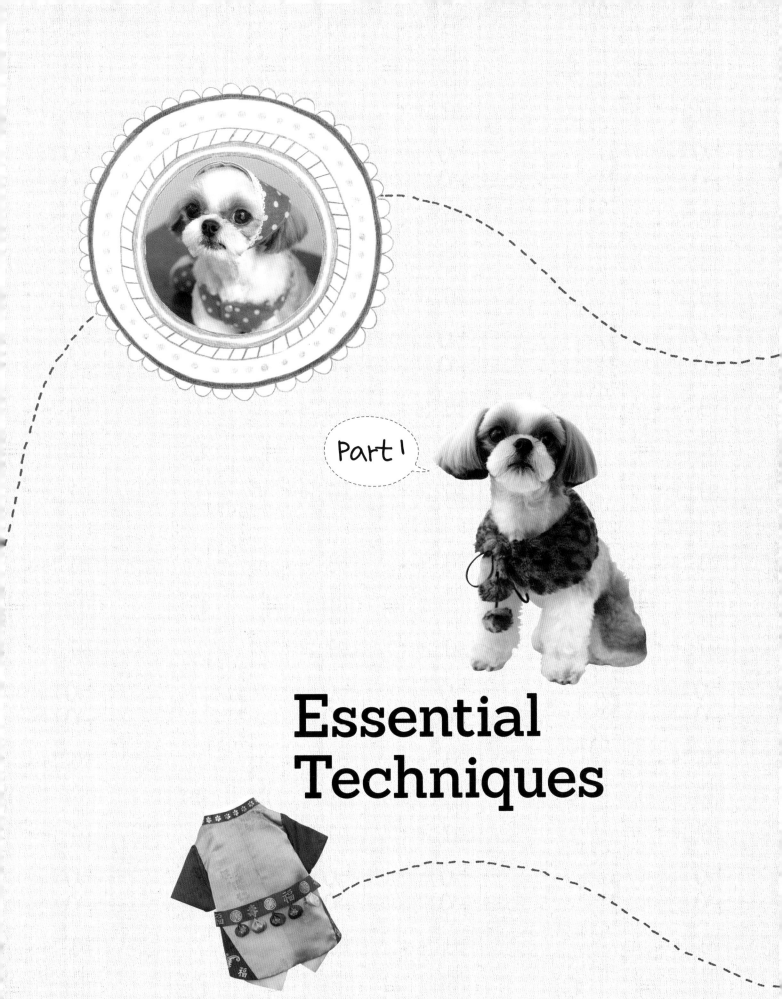

Part 1

Essential
Techniques

What You Need to Know Before You Begin

1 Understand the lengthwise and crosswise grain

While sewing clothes, the selvedge edge marks the lengthwise (vertical) grain of the fabric. This grain is more stable, so fabric should be cut along the lengthwise grain. A simple way to find the orientation of the fabric is to pull it. The lengthwise grain offers no elasticity while the crosswise (horizontal) grain has a bit of give. The fabric widths mentioned in this book and at your local fabric store refer to the horizontal width of the fabric. Make sure you are purchasing the right yardage for the specific width you find when gathering your supplies.

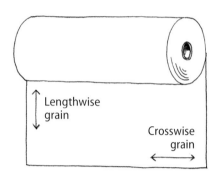

Lengthwise grain

Crosswise grain

2 Wash your fabric

Before you use your fabric, make sure to wash it so it preshrinks and behaves more like the natural fiber. To wash your fabric, soak it in warm water for 1 to 2 hours. Agitate it several times, then wring it out. Put it in a shady, cool place to air dry, then iron it when it is nearly dry.

3 Iron your fabric

Before you cut your fabric, I suggest that you iron it. Ironing your fabric before making clothes can improve the finished look. You should also iron your fabric at every step in the sewing process to make the seams more finished and the completed project look more professional.

4 Ways to cut your fabric

Unfolded fabric:

- Spread out the fabric with the wrong side up. Lay out the pattern pieces with the grain line aligned with the selvedge edge. Trace the pattern onto the fabric with marking tools, such as water-soluble pens, disappearing ink pens, or tailor's chalk.

- Trace around the pattern pieces for one side, then flip the pattern over to draw the remaining side.

- When flipping the pattern, make sure that the center marking is aligned. If the pattern calls for a center seam, make sure the necessary seam allowances are marked.

- Draw the necessary seam allowances with a seam gauge, then cut out the pattern pieces.

Half-folded fabric:

- Lay the pattern pieces on the half-folded fabric, then trace the pattern.

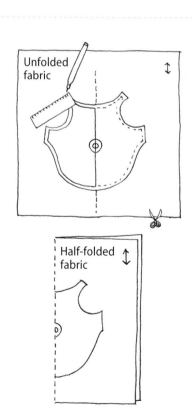

Unfolded fabric

Half-folded fabric

1 Measure your dog

Before you start making pet clothes, you need to know your dog's neck and chest circumferences. Since there might be measurement errors due to the dog's postures and different reference points, you need to confirm the measurements repeatedly according to the types of clothes you want to make.

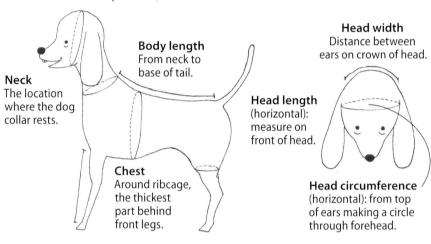

Head circumference (vertical)
From chin to top of head, in front of ears.

Neck
The location where the dog collar rests.

Body length
From neck to base of tail.

Chest
Around ribcage, the thickest part behind front legs.

Head width
Distance between ears on crown of head.

Head length (horizontal): measure on front of head.

Head circumference (horizontal): from top of ears making a circle through forehead.

Tips for measuring your dog

- Avoid measuring your dog while he leans to one side or looks down. Measure your dog while he stretches his back. Repeat several times and take an average.
- Avoid getting too tight or too loose when using the tape measure.
- Add a bit of extra length when measuring shaggy dogs.

Dog Clothing Size Chart (based on body length)

Size	Neck	Chest	Back length
XS	7½" (19cm)	11" (28cm)	8¾" (22cm)
S	8¾" (22cm)	12¾" (32cm)	9¾" (25cm)
M	9¾" (25cm)	14½" (37cm)	10½" (27cm)
L	11½" (29cm)	16½" (42cm)	11½" (29cm)
XL	13" (33cm)	19" (48cm)	13" (33cm)

Dog Hat Size Chart (based on body length)

Size	Head (horizontal)	Head (vertical)
S	8¼"–9¾" (21–25cm)	8¼"–9¾" (21–25cm)
M	10¼"–11¾" (26–30cm)	10¼"–11¾" (26–30cm)
L	12¼"–13¾" (31–35cm)	12¼"–13¾" (31–35cm)

- This chart is based on the dog's body length. The patterns in this book also follow this chart. You can use it as a reference to choose the patterns that best fit your dog.

- Using the same pattern with different fabrics might result in different sizes of the finished clothes. If you use thick materials like wools, be sure to add ¾"–1¼" (2–3cm) to the original patterns. On the other hand, if using knit fabric, you should subtract ⅜" (1cm) from the original patterns.

- The size of the front pieces will vary due to the dog gender. For female dogs, you can make the front pieces a bit shorter.

2 Find your pattern

Different kinds of dogs have different body types and sizes. Therefore it is impossible to have one-size-fits-all clothing for dogs. Before you copy and adjust the pattern, be sure you understand your dog's physical characteristics.

If the pattern fits...

- If any size (XS, S, M, L, XL) pattern from this book fits your dog, you can copy the pattern onto tracing paper or any other transparent paper.

- Glue the pattern to cardboard to help you cut it out and to keep it in place while you cut your fabric.

If the pattern doesn't fit...

- First you need to know the differences between your dog's size and the chart on page 13, including chest circumference, neck circumference, and back length.

- Follow the instructions for "How to alter the pattern" on page 15 to change the size.

3 Making muslins and basting

Before making the actual garment, you can make a sample (muslin) first from scrap fabric or cast-off clothes to make sure the pattern fits. After adding the seam allowances, cut the pattern along the cutting line. Baste along the seam lines, then try the muslin on your dog. If it doesn't fit, find out which part you need to alter for the pattern. Basting not only helps you reduce waste, but also makes sewing with the final fabric an easier process.

4 Cut

Lay the pattern pieces on the wrong side of your fabric and trace the patterns. You will begin to see how the garment looks after stitching up all the pattern pieces. Remember to add seam allowances outside of the seam lines from the pattern. After drawing the seam lines and allowances, you can cut the fabric along the cutting lines, then get to sewing.

The pattern arrangements found on the project instructions pages are meant to conveniently illustrate the pattern pieces you need and in what fabrics. This isn't necessarily the exact pattern layout, as you should judge and lay the patterns carefully to waste as little fabric as possible.

5 Sew

When sewing your dog clothes, you can either use a sewing machine or sew by hand. In my opinion, the best way is to use both methods. It is better to use a sewing machine for large clothes, but sewing by hand is preferred for details and textures. For fabric that ravels easy along the raw edges, I suggest finishing the edges with the overlock function of the sewing machine, or you can hand sew overcast stitches if you don't have a sewing machine.

6 Confirm the pattern size

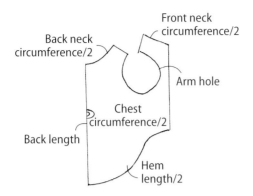

Front neck circumference/2

Back neck circumference/2

Arm hole

Chest circumference/2

Back length

Hem length/2

The figure on the left is an example of a half-folded pattern. Use a tape measure to check the size on each part, compare it to your dog's measurements, and decide whether you need to alter the pattern.

- Neck circumference = (back neck circumference/2+front neck circumference/2) x2
- Chest circumference = (chest circumference/2) x2
- Back length = back length
- Arm hole = arm hole
- Hem length = (hem length/2) x2

7 How to alter the pattern

No matter whether you want to make the pattern longer or shorter, you need to change the size of each pattern piece evenly.

1. If you need to lengthen both the chest and neck circumferences:
You can add width to the center front and back lines, or vertically cut the neckline open and spread it out (known as slashing and spreading).

2. If you need to shorten both the chest and neck circumferences:
You can trim the width of the center front and back lines, or vertically cut the neckline open and overlap the cut pieces to reduce the length.

3. If you need to lengthen both the chest circumference and the arm hole:
You can add width to the side seams of the front and back pieces, or slash and spread the arm hole.

4. If you need to shorten both the chest circumference and the arm hole:
You can trim the side seams, reducing the width of the front and back pieces, or vertically cut the armhole open and overlap the cut pieces to reduce the length.

5. If you need to lengthen both the neck circumference and the arm hole:
You can just lengthen the shoulder line.

6. If you need to shorten both the neck circumference and the arm hole:
You can just reduce the shoulder line.

7. If you need to lengthen the back length:
You can slash the pattern along the width, right under the arm hole, then spread the cut pieces adding another layer of paper underneath to bridge the gap.

8. If you need to shorten the back length:
You can slash the pattern along the width, right under the armhole, then overlap the cut pieces to reduce the length.

9. If you only need to lengthen the neck circumference:
Extend the neckline outward, then connect the line back to the shoulder line.

10. If you only need to shorten the neck circumference:
Trim the neckline inward, making sure it connects back to the shoulder line.

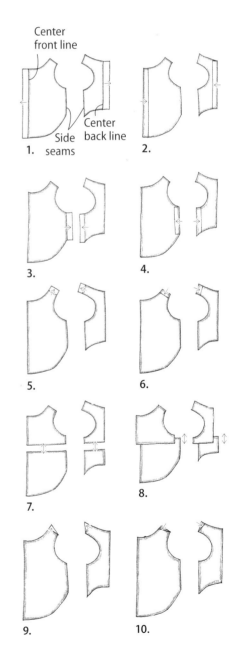

Center front line

Center back line

Side seams

1. 2. 3. 4. 5. 6. 7. 8. 9. 10.

Tools and Materials

1. **Seam gauge:** a ruler that shows various seam allowances. It is essential for sewing.

2. **Stitching awl:** to pick out fabric at edges or corners when turning the fabric right side out. Especially helpful for making thin ropes or straps. You can also use it to push or hold your fabric while underneath the sewing machine and protect your fingers.

3. **Seam ripper:** to rip seams when you make mistakes.

4. **Thimble:** to protect your fingertips from being poked by needles and to help you push needles easily while sewing with thicker fabric by hand.

5. **Scissors:** I suggest using dedicated scissors for different things: to cut fabric, use fabric scissors; to cut threads, use thread cutting scissors.

6. **Needles:** You will need different sizes of needles for different kinds of fabrics and uses. It's best to collect all kinds of sizes of sewing needles for both hand and machine sewing.

7. **Fabric markers:** a tool for tracing patterns or to mark size notes on the fabric. The ink of disappearing ink pens will evaporate in the air after a while, while the ink of water-soluble pens can be removed with water.

8. **Pins and pincushion:** pins are used to hold fabrics and notions in place while cutting or sewing. A pincushion is just the pin holder, commonly seen in two types: classic cushions and magnetic ones.

9. **Iron:** to smooth out your fabric or press creases along seam lines. You can iron the fabric before cutting and after finishing sewing.

10. **Tape measure:** to measure body size and curve lengths.

11. **Bone folder:** a very convenient tool used to mark seam allowances or fold lines.

12. **Tracing wheel:** a marking tool used to make dotted lines directly on patterns or fabric.

13. **Fabric adhesive:** a water-soluble glue for fabric. It can be used to hold fabric pieces together temporarily as a substitute for pins. You can also use it to glue pockets on clothes.

1. **Thread:** comes in different types, including cotton and silk threads, and in a variety of colors. I recommend choosing one in a similar material as your fabric and in a color a shade darker than the fabric. Make sure you use hand-sewing threads while sewing by hand since these threads are very strong and do not easily break.

2. **Basting threads for quilting:** General basting threads break easily, but basting thread for quilting is made from 100% cotton, is soft and doesn't tangle easily, and is a better choice for both quilting and basting.

3. **Invisible threads:** transparent and thin, this thread is used to hide stitches.

4. **Embroidery threads:** thicker than regular threads, these can be used to embroider patterns or for decorative stitches.

5. **Hook-and-loop fastener:** a fabric fastener using by sticking the loop side to the hooked side. This makes sizing adjustable in clothing.

6. **Leather cording:** used to decorate bags or accessories.

7. **Cotton strings:** used to decorate accessories by tying on beads or by knotting.

8. **Elastic:** used to make the size of clothes or hats adjustable. Be sure to pick the proper size according to the project instructions.

9. **Loop turner:** used to turn long straps inside out. The handle and hook design makes it very easy to use.

10. **Bodkin needle:** used to draw elastic or cotton strings through thin tubes or similar casings.

11. **Fusible stay tape:** also known as fusible stabilizing tape, these tapes are available in a wide variety. Choose the proper one according to the fabric you're using and the final use of the finished product. To use it, put the stay tape on top of the fabric with the glue facing down and iron it. The benefit of the stay tape is to prevent curved edges from becoming stretched out or warped. It helps the overall shape of the garment and improves the finished look.

12. **Locking forceps:** a tool that helps fill projects with batting. It is especially convenient for tucking batting and other fillings into narrow openings.

13. **Polyester fiberfill:** a kind of filling material that quickly restores to its original shape and doesn't easily bunch after being washed. It is commonly used to fill dolls and accessories.

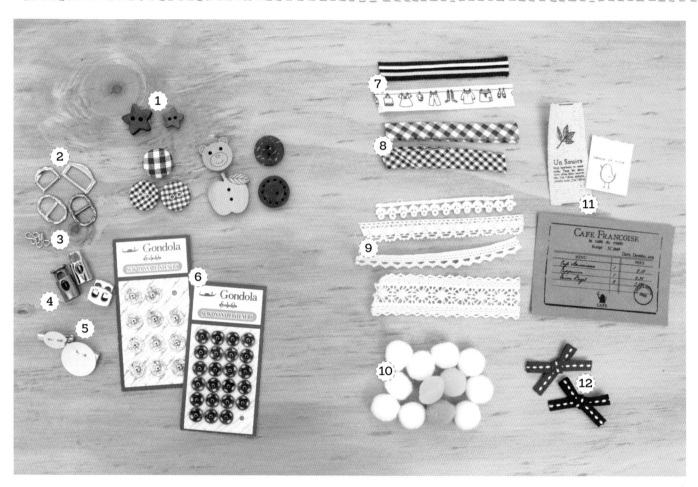

1. **Decorative buttons:** available in various styles and materials. You can enhance the look of a finished product.

2. **Slide buckles and D-rings:** inserting a belt onto a slide buckle can make the belt length adjustable. Be sure you choose the proper hardware according to your project. D-rings are typically used as joiners on hats or bags, and, unlike slide buckles, you need to sew D-rings onto straps or belts.

3. **Hook and eye:** a hook-and-eye closure is a very simple and secure method of fastening garments together. It can be used on skirts, dresses, cardigans, vests, and capes. There are two parts of this fastening item—a hook and an eye. You need to sew them on as a pair.

4. **Spring stopper:** the length of your cording can be adjustable after putting it through a spring stopper. They can be made from metal or plastic.

5. **Brooch base:** you can create a brooch just by gluing some decorative ribbons and buttons onto a brooch base with hot glue adhesive.

6. **Invisible snaps:** An invisible snap comes in a pair—a prong and socket. They can be used as a substitute for regular buttons, but be sure to confirm the placement before sewing them on.

7. **Decorative ribbons:** items to enhance the style of bags and accessories. Don't forget to choose ones that match the material of your project.

8. **Bias tape:** available in various sizes and materials, such as linen, cotton and knit. You can choose a suitable one based on your project needs, or you can make them yourself from your own fabric.

9. **Lace strips:** suitable for all kinds of fabrics and designs. There are many sizes and patterns. You should keep a variety of them handy.

10. **Pom-poms:** available in a wide variety of sizes and colors. They can be used as decorations or as substitutes for buttons.

11. **Fabric labels:** sewn on the finished products to make them more recognizable. There are many sizes and patterns. You should keep a variety of them handy.

12. **Bows:** suitable for decorating clothes and accessories. You can attach them with stitching or hot glue adhesive.

Fabrics

1. **Cotton/linen blend:** While making pet clothes, it is better to use a cotton/linen blend than 100% pure linen because it is softer and more resilient. When making clothes, washed linen is recommended; when making accessories, you can use thicker linen fabrics.

2. **Stretch cotton:** soft and with high absorbency. However, sewing with it is challenging for beginners because it can shift while sewing. Seams can also pop when the fabric stretches, so sewing with a serger (overlocker) is needed.

3. **Pure cotton:** the yarn count represents the thickness of the threads used for weaving the fabric. The higher the number, the finer the thread is. For dogs with sensitive skin, fabric with a higher count is recommended.

4. **Quilting fabric:** there are fabrics suitable for quilting available in many stores. It is very convenient to use.

5. **Silk:** soft and thin, silk is usually used to make scarves or ties.

6. **Flannelette, single and double napped:** Flannelette is famous for its softness, breathability, and absorbability, and is commonly used for baby clothes. Double-napped flannelette has a nap on both sides of the fabric, and is used for handkerchiefs and scarves.

7. **Organic terrycloth and terrycloth without fluorescent agent:** Since there is no chemical added in the production process, this type of fabric is suitable to make leisure clothes and toys for dogs with sensitive skin.

8. **Terrycloth:** you can choose different thicknesses and loop lengths according to the usage. If you want to make bath products, terrycloth with loops on both sides is recommended.

9. **Padded microfiber:** soft and padded, usually used to make cushions and beddings.

10. **Leather and denim:** these have great stability and are easy to use. You can sew them directly on the right side of the fabric; they often look their best with topstitching.

11. **Microfiber double-sided fleece:** soft and comfortable. With fleece on both sides, it is suitable for winter clothes and hats.

12. **Double-sided coating cloth:** although it is waterproof, this will still get wet after soaking in water for too long, because it is not woven by 100% polyethylene.

Basic Sewing Terminology

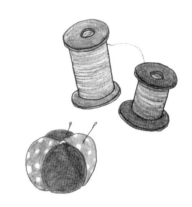

1 Seam allowance
The width between the seam line and the cutting line marked on the fabric after tracing the pattern.

2 Edge stitching
A stitch that is sewn on the right side of the outer fabric after stitching it to another piece of fabric. It is a sewing technique that prevents the project from looking bulky, or is used for decorative purposes. Stitch 1/16" to 1/8" (0.2–0.3cm) in from the finished seam. Sew very carefully when doing edge stitching. Sewing further out from the edge, about 1/4" to 3/8" (0.5–1cm), is known as topstitching.

3 Opening for turning
A section on the seam line left open for turning the project right side out when the rest of the garment or lining is sewn. The smaller the opening the better, as long as the project can still be turned inside out. After turning the project right side out, a blind stitch is commonly used to close the opening, or sometimes an edge stitch is used for a decorative seam finish.

4 Clipping and notching
After sewing the fabric pieces up but before turning the project right side out, we usually cut small notches with consistent spacing in the seam allowance to flatten the seam, especially on the curves (for concave curves, clip; for convex curves, notch). To prevent the seam allowances from overlapping, getting creased, or being too thick, clipping seam allowance at corners is also recommended. Be careful not to cut into your stitches. If you are using stretch fabrics, you can trim the width of the seam allowance instead of notching and clipping.

5 Filling
Carefully use the locking forceps to stuff the batting in. When the filling process is almost done, slowly close the opening with blind stitching while pushing in more filling to avoid uneven filling and to ensure a smooth seam finish.

Tip

Natural fiberfill and polyester fiberfill
There are two kinds of synthetic fiberfill commercially available: natural fiberfill and polyester fiberfill. Polyester fiberfill has better resilience and fluffiness. It is not easily bunched up, so it is commonly used to fill dolls and accessories. When filling larger projects, such as pillows and cushions, we usually use natural fiberfill. I suggest you to choose the best fiberfill based the project instructions and the intended use of the project.

Natural fiberfill   Polyester fiberfill

Basic Sewing Techniques

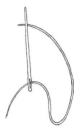 **1**   ## Knotting the thread

 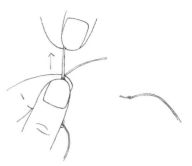

1. Lay the sharp end of the needle on top of one end of the thread.

2. Wrap the thread around the needle 2–3 times.

3. Grip the wrapped thread with your thumb and index finger. Pull the needle with the other hand while maintaining your grip until the wrapped thread becomes a tight knot.

 **2**   ## Basic stitches

Running stitch: used to stitch two pieces of fabric together or for a decorative topstitch.

 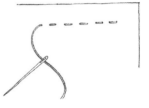

1. After knotting the thread, pull the needle through the fabric from the wrong side to the right side.

2. Make your stitches about ¹⁄₁₆"–⅛" (0.2–0.3cm) apart.

3. Weave your needle in and out for about 3 to 4 stitches then pull the needle all the way through the fabric.

Back stitch: a stronger and more secure stitch than a running stitch.

1. After knotting the thread, bring the needle through the fabric to the right side.

2. Make one stitch, then pull the needle through the fabric.

3. Create one more stitch by going back to where the needle emerged previously. Pull the needle through the fabric.

4. Repeat steps 2 and 3.

Overcast stitch: used as a seam finish to prevent raveling, or as a hem finish.

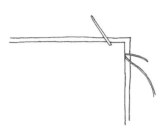  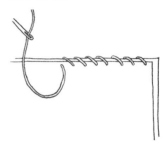

1. After knotting the thread, bring the needle through the fabric to the top edge.

2. Insert the needle diagonally from the inner edge of the fabric and bring it out on the right side.

3. Repeat accordingly until reaching the end. Knot the thread at the end of the stitching line.

Blind stitch: used to secure hems or to close the opening for turning.

 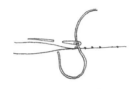 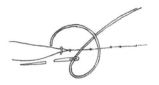

1. After knotting the thread, insert the needle from the wrong side of the fabric and bring it out on the right side.

2. Pull the thread out and take a stitch on the seam allowance.

3. Don't pull the thread too tight while sewing. Make every effort to ensure that the stitches are hidden inside.

Basting stitch: a temporary stitch to hold the pieces of fabric together or to secure the outer fabric and lining in place before making the actual seam.

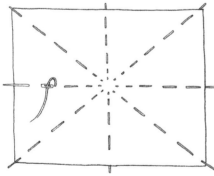

On the fabric, baste along the horizontal, vertical and diagonal lines that cross in the center. There is no need to secure the thread after stitching, but rather leave a 2–2⅜" (5–6cm) thread tail at the end. After finishing the actual stitches, pull out the basting thread.

Embroidery: sewing with embroidery and colorful silk threads for decorative purposes.

Running stitch: a decorative stitch on the right side of the fabric, same as the running stitch in sewing.

Back stitch: a decorative stitch to show the embroidery threads on the right side, same as the back stitch in sewing.

3 Seam finishing techniques

Plain seam finish: Press the seam allowances open for both pieces of the fabric after sewing.

(wrong side)

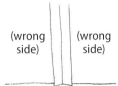

(wrong side) (wrong side)

1. With right sides facing, stitch the two pieces of the fabric.

2. Press the seam allowances open and iron them flat.

Reversed seam finish: Press the seam allowances of both pieces toward the same side.

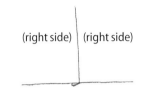

(wrong side) (wrong side)

(right side) (right side)

1. With right sides facing, stitch the two pieces of the fabric.

2. Press both seam allowances toward the same side.

Flat fell seam finish: Wrap one side of the seam allowance around the other side then edge stitch the fold in place.

(wrong side) (wrong side)

1. After stitching, trim one of the seam allowances.

(wrong side) (wrong side)

2. Fold the untrimmed seam allowance, wrap the trimmed seam allowance inside and press. Edge stitch the folded edge.

How to prevent raveling

To prevent raveling at the fabric edge, you can use the overlock function or zigzag stitches with your sewing machine, or sew overcast stitches by hand.

Overlocking

Zigzag stitch

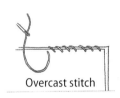

Overcast stitch

---

4 Hem finishing techniques

Single-fold hem

(right side) (wrong side)

This is the most basic hem finishing technique. After the raw edge of the fabric is finished (with overlocking, zigzag, or overcasting stitches), make a single fold and press. Sew the hem in place directly from the right side of the fabric.

Double-fold hem

(right side) (wrong side)

With this method, the raw edge finish is not needed. Make two folds on the edge of the fabric, then press them in place. Sew the hem in place directly from the right side of the fabric.

5 Bound seam finish techniques

Making bias tape

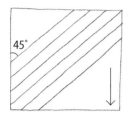

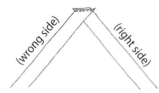

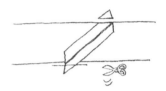

1. On the fabric, draw diagonal lines across the fabric, 1⅜" (3.5cm) apart. Cut all of the strips.

2. Put every 2 strips together with right sides facing at right angles. Mark the seam line, then sew them all together. (Tip: for stretch fabrics such as cotton interlock, it is easier to make binding tape along the crosswise grain.)

3. Use a plain seam finish for the seam allowances. Trim the opposite corners off.

Bound finish for a straight seam

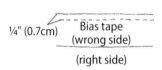

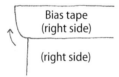

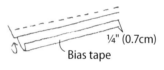

1. Align one edge of the bias tape and the fabric together with right sides facing, then sew them together.

2. Press the bias tape away from the main fabric, as if to wrap it around the seam allowance.

3. Fold the raw edge of the bias tape under just enough so that when folded over it covers the previous seam.

4. Fold the tape over, then blind stitch the bias tape in place. Be sure the stitches do not show. You can also edge stitch the tape in place.

Bound finish for a curved seam

1. Align one edge of the bias tape and the fabric together with right sides facing and pin them in place.

2. Stitch them together along the seam line.

3. Press the bias tape away from the main fabric, then fold under the raw edge of the bias tape inward just enough so that when folded over it covers the previous seam.

4. Fold the tape over, then blind stitch the bias tape in place. Be sure the stitches do not show. You can also sew it in place with an edge stitch on the right side of the fabric.

6   Making fabric straps

Folding method

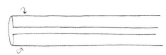

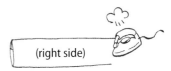
(right side)

1. Fold both sides of the fabric strip to the center with wrong sides together and press.

2. Fold the strip in half with wrong sides together. Iron it flat, then edge stitch along the folded edges.

Turning method

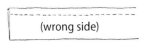
(wrong side)

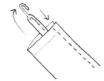
(right side)

1. Fold the fabric strip in half with right sides facing and sew.

2. Turn the strip right side out with a loop turner.

3. After turning the strip right side out, iron the strip, then edge stitch both sides.

7   Making decorative fabric-covered buttons

1. Cut a round piece of the fabric large enough to cover the entire button completely. Sew a running stitch along the inner edge of the fabric. Don't cut the thread after stitching.

2. Put the button in the middle of the stitched fabric piece. Pull the ends of the thread until the fabric gathers up and wraps around the button.

3. Carefully clean up the back side of the button.

8   Gathering fabric

By hand

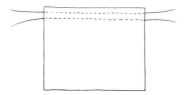

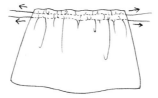

1. Sew two running stitch seams along the edge, leaving a 4–6" (10–15cm) thread tail at both ends.

2. Match up the center of your fabric with your main project, then pull the threads to gather the fabric towards the middle. Make slight adjustments so the fabric is the size you need.

By machine

You can gather fabric by machine by lengthening your machine stitch or by using a gathering foot directly on the fabric edge.

Basic knitting and crocheting

The needleworking projects introduced in this book (Knitted Cape on page 84, Hat with Scarf on page 87) only require basic knitting and crocheting skills. By making yourself familiar with these basics, you can easily complete those projects.

Gauge swatch

Knitting or crocheting a small sample can show the number of stitches and rows in a 4" by 4" (10 x 10cm) area. The gauge needed varies from pattern to pattern, and the gauge you result in can depend on the size of the yarn and needles.

- Before knitting/crocheting your project, make a 6" by 6" (15 x 15cm) square with your yarn and crochet hook or knitting needles.

- Spread the piece flat with your palms, then iron.

- Count the number of stitches and rows in a 4" by 4" (10 x 10cm) area.

- Compare this to the gauge required for your project. Increase or decrease the size of your needles/hook accordingly.

Basic knitting skills

Knit stitch   Purl stitch

Basic knitting chart stitches

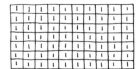

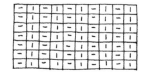

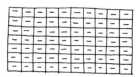

Stockinette stitch: the most basic knitting pattern. Knit on every right side row, then purl on every wrong side row. It is stretchable.

Knit one, purl one ribbing: alternating knitting and purling in every other stitch. Mostly used to make up the hems, necks, and cuffs of sweaters.

Reverse stockinette stitch: the back side of stockinette stitch.

Basic crochet stitches

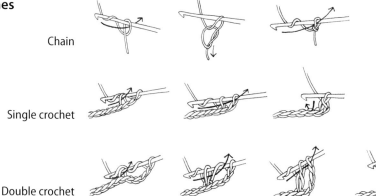

Chain

Single crochet

Double crochet

How to Use This Book

Each project in this book is presented with every detail necessary to create the project, even for a novice sewer.

Button-Down Shirt

SIZES	XS through XL
FABRIC	⅓–⅔ yd. (⅓–⅔m) of plaid cotton
NOTIONS	Invisible or pearl snaps ¼ yd. (¼m) of lightweight fusible interfacing

 A

 B

1 **Cut the fabric pattern pieces out.** Lay the pattern pieces on the wrong side of the fabric and trace around the pieces, adding a ⅜" (1cm) seam allowance, except for the hems, which require a ¾" (2cm) seam allowance. Cut out the fabric, then cut two collar pieces from the fusible interfacing. Iron the interfacing to the wrong side of the collar pieces.

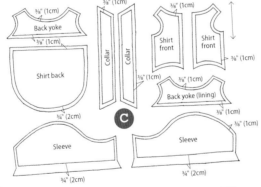

⅜" (1cm) Back yoke
⅜" (1cm)
Shirt back
¾" (2cm)
Collar   Collar
Shirt front   Shirt front
⅜" (1cm)
Back yoke (lining)
⅜" (1cm)
⅜" (1cm)
Sleeve   Sleeve
¾" (2cm)   ¾" (2cm)

C

 **D**

2 **Join the back to the back yoke pieces.** Layer the straight edge of the shirt back between the two yoke pieces with right sides facing. Sew the three layers together, then press the seam allowance toward the back yoke. Edge stitch the previous seam.

3 **Interface the placket front.** Cut strips of interfacing wide enough to cover the shirt plackets found along the center front of the shirt front pieces. Iron the fusible interfacing to the wrong side of the placket.

A. Opening each project are model shots of a happy dog wearing the completed projects. These shots are a handy reference when you are putting together your project. They help you see what you're aiming to create and how the piece should fit your dog.

B. Each project instructions section starts off with the essentials you need to know. These include the finished size of the project used for the instructions, the amount and type of fabric you'll need to buy, and a list of additional notions you'll need like buttons, interfacing, and other bits and pieces.

C. Next, you see the pattern pieces and their essential measurements so that you can cut out all your pieces. Many full-size patterns, some shown in sizes XS-XL, are available in the pattern pack; some rectangular pieces you can measure and cut out yourself.

D. Finally, you can follow the clear photographs, illustrations, and step-by-step instructions to put together your selected project. Tips throughout help ensure that you don't miss a detail.

bow-wow

Meet the Dogs

Ari

Breed: Shih Tzu
Age: 5
Gender: F
Characteristics: She is a short-haired girl with a pair of bright and intelligent eyes, a pair of long legs, and a charming S-curved figure. Her personality, however, is like a tomboy. But sometimes she can also be affectionate, tender, and soft. It totally depends on her mood.

See more Ari! GoGo!

blog.naver.com/naanhye8098

A-Dong

Breed: English Cocker Spaniel
Age: 9
Gender: F
Characteristics: She has a sincere appearance and a gentle personality. She is very intelligent, like a model student: even without special training, she knows what to do. She is very into soccer balls.

See more A-Dong! GoGo!

blog.naver.com/mn1853

Little Nine

Breed: Yorkie
Age: 9
Gender: M
Characteristics: He thinks he is human and is very polite: before going into a room, he will knock on the door first. His likes to peek in on his mom while she puts on makeup. His favorite things are chicken brisket jerky and his elder sister Totto.

See more Little Nine! GoGo!

fullmoon1977.blog.me

Natto

Breed: Maltese
Age: 2
Gender: M
Characteristics: He is a little devil in angel's clothing. Even though he has an innocent appearance, he is actually a troublemaker! But he always treats his little sister as a friend. He is good at biting off dolls' noses.

See more Natto! Go^{Go!}

fullmoon1977.blog.me

Chiu-Chiu

Breed: Shih Tzu
Age: 8
Gender: F
Characteristics: With a naïve and romantic personality, Chiu-Chiu likes to make friends with people and dogs. When it comes time for a stroll, she happily jumps around like a rabbit. She is so timid that she is afraid of plastic bags. When taking a stroll, however, she fears nothing and no one!

Do-Do

Breed: Shih Tzu
Age: 3
Gender: F
Characteristics: She is tame and cute, moving slowly as sloth. She is considered one of the best toy lovers among dogs!

Little Moon

Breed: Maltese
Age: 3
Gender: F
Characteristics: With spotless soft white hairs all over her body, a slender body shape, and bright and intelligent eyes, Little Moon is veritably a beauty among dogs. She doesn't look very easygoing, but she is actually naughty and playful. She loves eating and teasing her younger brother, Little Star.

See more Little Moon! Go^{Go!}

blog.naver.com/83187love

Milu

Breed: Mini Dobermann
Age: 5
Gender: M
Characteristics: He often stares at his dad, whining to get snacks. If he finishes up the snacks in his bowl, he will look very sad. He is a master of acting pitiful.

See more Milu! GoGo!
blog.naver.com/hjh9313

Little Sky

Breed: Yorkie
Age: 5
Gender: F
Characteristics: This little lady likes to play ball and act affectionate. Sometimes she runs totally wild. She loves going for walks so much that she has become head of the neighborhood. Although she is small, she has a loud voice, which often makes her owner lose face!

See more Little Sky! GoGo!
blog.naver.com/pingsun2

Aroya

Breed: Maltese
Age: 5
Gender: F
Characteristics: With a pair of dark liquid eyes, beautiful double-fold eyelids, and a long, smooth tail, she looks innocent and lovely. Although she looks a bit unfriendly, as soon as Aroya glances back, anyone will have a crush on her.

See more Aroya! GoGo!
Celebelin.blog.mew

Pully

Breed: Toy Poodle
Age: 7
Gender: F
Characteristics: She is a master of being affectionate and sometimes of acting up and making trouble. But actually Pully is very clever and considerate, as long as she is able to be out for a walk every day. Her mom and her elder sister can tell she is very happy just through her eyes.

See more Pully! GoGo!
blog.naver.com/jjrs

Gucci

Breed: Yorkie
Age: 8
Gender: F
Characteristics: She likes to play with balls—probably 99.9% of her brain is thinking ball, ball, ball, and ball. As soon as she sees a ball, she will chase after it regardless of danger. Although she is not that affectionate, she still wins our hearts with her easygoing and honest personality.

See more Gucci! GoGo!

blog.naver.com/tingk70

Dor Kong

Breed: Shih Tzu
Age: 3
Gender: M
Characteristics: When Dor Kong was still a baby, because his front teeth didn't come in for a long time, his mom often massaged his gums with her fingers. One time he gently bit his mom's fingers. This is probably his way of showing his affection. He hates to leave his mom and is always clinging to her like chewing gum.

See more Dor Kong GoGo!

blog.naver.com/der_nachhall

Furryhead

Breed: Yorkie
Age: 9
Gender: M
Characteristics: He shows his preferences clearly and was born with rude manners. He is well known as "Malingering Devil King" in the animal hospital. His way of getting attention is to put his tongue out and express innocence in his eyes.

See more Furryhead! GoGo!

blog.naver.com/tingk70

Fei-Fei

Breed: Toy Poodle
Age: 3
Gender: F
Characteristics: Her interest is running! If a national running race is ever held, Fei-Fei will win first place. Her appearance often gives a mistaken impression of being taciturn, but she is actually very lively and outgoing.

See more Fei-Fei! GoGo!

yourlucia.blog.me

Part 2

Projects

Soft and comfy

Leisure Top

This style of leisurewear is made of soft and comfortable fabric specially designed for dogs with sensitive skin. Because the fabric is very flexible, wearing it will not affect the dog's daily activities. In addition, the fabric will keep dogs warm, so it is suitable for dogs that cannot bear the chill of fall and winter.

♥ You can use the same fabric
as the top to make a matching
bow barrette.

Leisure Top

SIZES	XS through XL
FABRIC	⅓–½ yd. (⅓–½m) of non-fluorescent French terry knit with a cartoon pattern
NOTIONS	1¼–2 yd. (1¼–2m) of ⅜" (1cm) wide decorative lace 3½" (9cm) of 1" (2.5cm) wide decorative lace Three ⅜" (1cm) wide wooden buttons

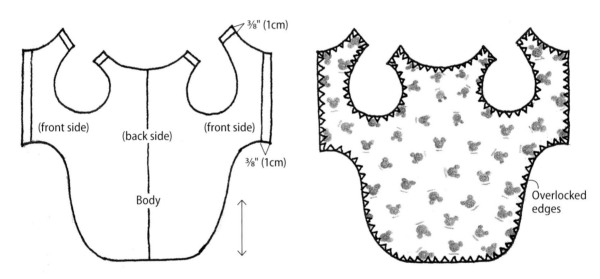

3/8" (1cm)

(front side) (back side) (front side)

3/8" (1cm)

Body

Overlocked edges

1 **Cut the fabric pattern pieces out.** Lay the pattern pieces on the wrong side of the fabric and trace the pattern. Add ⅜" (1cm) seam allowance at the shoulder and center front seams. Cut out the fabric pieces, then overlock the edges.

2 **Stitch the shoulder seam and center front.** Align the shoulder seams of the fabric pieces together with right sides facing. Pin and sew them in place. Similarly, align the center front edges of the fabric with right sides facing, then pin and sew them together.

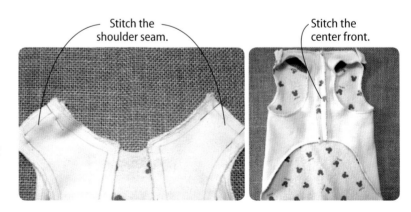

Stitch the shoulder seam.

Stitch the center front.

3 **Add lace trim on the collar.** Apply the lace over the neck opening to cover the overlocking stitches. When you reach the starting point again, overlap the ends of the lace, cut the excess, and edge stitch on the overlap to finish the seam.

The best starting point when sewing the lace is the intersection of the seam allowances.

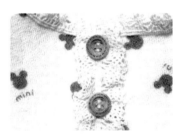

Sew lace trim on the collar.

Sew lace trim on the armholes.

Sew lace trim on the hem.

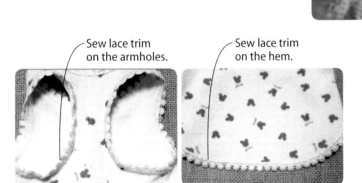

4 **Add lace trim on the armholes and hem.** As in step 3, sew lace along the armholes and hem.

5 **Attach lace and buttons to the center back.** Fold under the short ends of the lace strip, then sew it on the center back of the shirt with a shorter stitch. Attach the buttons to finish.

I'm a cuty girl~

Hooded Cloak

This cloak with a hood is very easy to put on and to take off. Just put it around your dog's neck, tie a beautiful bow, and voilà! Your dog looks perfectly cute!

Just looking at my back, can't you see how fashionable I am?

♥ Just put the cloak around your dog's neck, tie a beautiful bow, and you're done!

Hooded Cloak

SIZES	XS through XL
FABRIC	¼–½ yd. (¼–½m) of thin denim for outer cloak
	¼–½yd. (¼–½m) of dyed jacquard linen for lining
NOTIONS	1–1⅔ yd. (1–1⅔m) of wide white lace for hem
	⅔–1 yd. (⅔–1m) of blue lace for hood
	1" (2.5cm) tab of hook-and-loop fastener

Cut the fabric pattern pieces out. Lay the pattern pieces on the wrong side of the fabric and trace the pattern. Add a ⅜" (1cm) seam allowance on all the edges except for a ⅝" (1.5cm) seam allowance along the long edges of the ruffle hem. Cut the fabric pieces out.

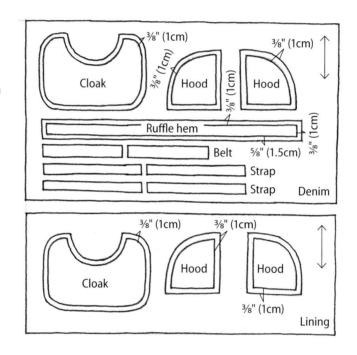

Lace

Add ruffles to the cloak hem. Make a double-fold hem along one long edge of the ruffled hem piece. Baste the white lace over the ruffled hem piece, then run gathering stitches along the top of both layers. Gather the hem evenly until its length matches the rounded outer edge of the cloak. After gathering, pin it to the edge of the cloak with right sides facing, then sew it in place.

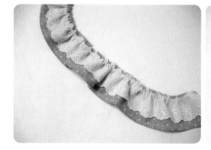

3 **Make the belt and the straps.** Layer two strap pieces with right sides facing and sew them together along the sides and one long edge, leaving the remaining long edge open. Trim the corners and seam allowances, then turn the strap right side out. Tuck under the seam allowances from the opening, then edge stitch the folded edges. Sew the belt pieces similarly.

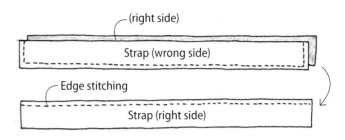

(right side)

Strap (wrong side)

Edge stitching

Strap (right side)

Cut notches.

Outer hood

Make two sets of edge stitches along each side of the center hood seam.

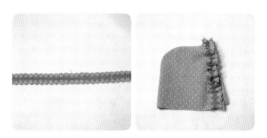

4 **Make the hood.** Layer the two hood pieces together with right sides facing and sew them along the curved edge. Trim the seam allowance to ¼" (0.5cm) and cut notches in the curves. Press the seam open, then sew two sets of edge stitches along each side of the center hood seam. Repeat this same step with the hood lining.

5 **Prepare the lace trim for the hood.** Gather the lace until it's shortened to the length of the hood front edge. Baste only the ends of the gathered lace along the bottom corners of the outer hood fabric.

6 **Join the cloak and hood.** Align the bottom edge of the hood with the upper curved edge of the cloak where the neck seam will be. Sew them together, then repeat this with the lining pieces.

Lining

Shell

7 **Attach the belt and straps.** Line each strap end up at the upper corners of the cloak, and the belt piece along one bottom corner. Baste the straps and belt in place.

Belt

Straps

8 **Join the outer cloak and lining.** Layer the outer cloak and lining with right sides facing, lining up all the raw edges. Sew the two together, leaving a 4" (10cm) opening for turning right side out, and being sure not to let the straps or belt get in the way or get sewn accidentally. Notch the seam allowances, then turn the cloak right side out.

9 **Sew the hood lace.** Line up the lace from the hood over the edge of the hood seam, letting some of the trim extend beyond the seam. Sew the lace in place, making two parallel seams along the middle of the lace for the best finish.

10 **Sew the outer cloak and attach the fastener.** Edge stitch along the bottom edge of the cloak, avoiding the hood, and closing up the opening. Sew the loop side of the hook-and-loop fastener on the bottom corner of the inner cloak (opposite the belt), and the hook side of the hook-and-loop fastener on the free end of the belt.

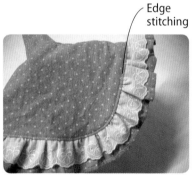

Edge stitching

Hook-and-loop fastener

Comfy Hoodie

Although dogs can stand cold weather better than human beings, putting a warm hoodie on your dog while walking in the cold air helps protect your dog. Remember to choose a soft and thick fabric for this project.

♥ You can also pull up the hood when it is windy outside.

Comfy Hoodie

SIZES	XS through XL
FABRIC	⅓–½ yd. (⅓–½m) of striped cotton interlock for outer hoodie
	¼–⅓ yd. (¼–⅓m) of 100% cotton interlock for hood lining
NOTIONS	Two wooden buttons
	Decorative fabric label
	⅔–1 yd. (⅔–1m) of cotton string for hoodie drawstring

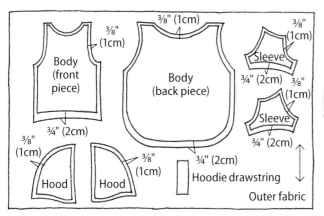
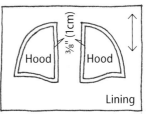

1 **Cut the fabric pattern pieces out.** Lay the pattern pieces on the wrong side of the fabric and trace the pattern. Add a ¾" (2cm) seam allowance for all the hems, and add a ⅜" (1cm) for the rest of the edges. Cut all the fabric pieces out.

2 **Join the front and back body pieces.** Align the front and back body pieces with right sides together along the side seams, matching up the stripes from the fabric. Sew them in place, then overlock the seam allowances. Press the seam allowances toward the hoodie front.

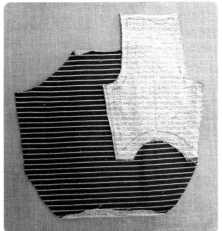

3 Make the sleeves, part 1.
Fold the left and right sleeve pieces in half, matching up the side seams. Sew the seams, then overlock the seam allowances and hems. Mark the hem fold line on the right side of the fabric.

4 Make the sleeves, part 2.
Fold the hem toward the wrong side, then press the fold in place. Topstitch it in place ⅝" and ⅛" (1.5 and 0.3cm) from the fold.

Press the hem.

5 Join the sleeves.
Mark the left and right sleeves, then line up the armhole seam with that of the hoodie body. Match up the side seams, pin the edges in place, then sew them together.

6 **Make the hoodie drawstring.** Fold the hoodie drawstring in half with wrong sides together. Tuck under the seam allowances and hand sew the drawstring with a blind stitch.

7 **Make the hood, part 1.** Put the two outer hood pieces together with right sides facing, then tuck the hoodie drawstring in between where the pattern guidelines indicate. Sew the hoodie pieces together along the top curved edge. Repeat this with the lining pieces, without the drawstring.

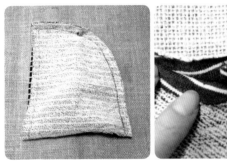

8 **Make the hood, part 2.** Layer the hood outer fabric and lining together with right sides facing and sew them together along the straight edge, leaving the neck seam open. Start ⅜" (1cm) from the beginning and stop short ⅜" (1cm) from the end. Turn the hood right side out and top stitch the previous seam, ⅜" (1cm) from the edge, to create a drawstring casing.

Stop short ⅜" (1cm) from the beginning and end of the seam at the corner of the neck.

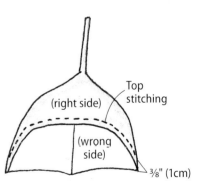

Top stitching

(right side)

(wrong side)

⅜" (1cm)

9 **Join the body and hood, part 1.** Align the neck seam of the hood with that of the body, right sides facing. Pin the body to just the outer hood and not the lining. For the front corners of the hood, find the center of the body front along the neckline, then overlap the hood corners by ¼" (0.5cm) at the center. When everything is properly pinned, sew around the perimeter of the neckline.

10 **Join the body and hood, part 2.** Iron the seam allowance toward the hood, then fold under the seam allowance from the lining. Layer it over the previous neck seam, then edge stitch the fold in place from the right side of the garment.

11 **Sew the hem.** Finish the raw edge of the hem with overlock stitches, then pull the threads to gather the fabric along the curves. Iron the hem flat, then top stitch in place twice with seams ⅝" and ⅛" (1.5 and 0.3cm) away from the fold.

 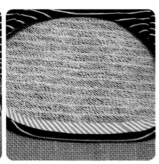

12 **Attach the hoodie drawstring, fabric label, and buttons.** Cut slits into the bottom corners of the drawstring casing (from step 8), about ¾" (2cm) up from the center front. Thread the cotton string through to finish the drawstring. Sew on the fabric label, then attach the wooden buttons to the ends of the drawstring for decoration.

Your dog can dry himself

Bathrobe

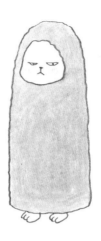

After a bath, put this bathrobe on your dog right after he shakes the water off. It will absorb the remaining water naturally while the dog wiggles and jiggles his body. This bathrobe also comes in handy after you play with your dog in the water.

♥ You can embroider some
cute patterns or your dog's
name on the bathrobe.

Bathrobe

SIZES	XS through XL
FABRIC	¼–⅔ yd. (¼–⅔m) of cotton double-sided terrycloth (⅛" [0.4cm] loop length)
NOTIONS	Red, blue, and yellow embroidery floss

1 **Cut the fabric pattern pieces out.** Lay the pattern pieces on the wrong side of the fabric and trace the pattern. Add a ⅜" (1cm) seam allowance around the edges and cut the fabric pieces out.

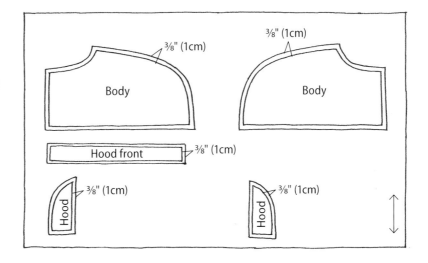

Body — ⅜" (1cm)   ⅜" (1cm) — Body

Hood front — ⅜" (1cm)

Hood — ⅜" (1cm)   Hood — ⅜" (1cm)

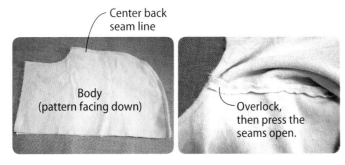

Center back seam line

Body (pattern facing down)

Overlock, then press the seams open.

2 **Join the body pieces.** Align the body pieces together with right sides facing and sew the center back seam (the curved back edge). Overlock the seam allowances, then press the seam open.

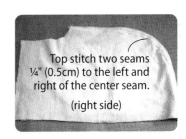

Top stitch two seams ¼" (0.5cm) to the left and right of the center seam.

(right side)

3 **Topstitch on the right side.** From the right side of the fabric, sew top stitching seams ¼" (0.5cm) to the left and right of the center back seam.

4 **Join the hood part 1.**
Align the two hood pieces with right sides together and sew the center back seam (the curved edge). Overlock the seam allowances, then press the seam open. From the right side of the fabric, sew top stitching seams ¼" (0.5cm) to the left and right of the center back seam.

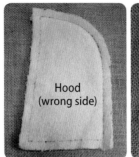

Hood (wrong side)

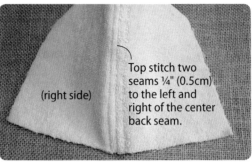

(right side)

Top stitch two seams ¼" (0.5cm) to the left and right of the center back seam.

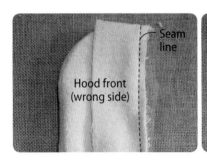

Hood front (wrong side)

Seam line

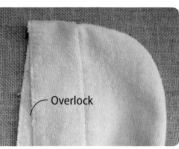

Overlock

Stitch the seam allowance of the hood.

5 **Join the hood, part 2.** Align the hood front piece along the straight edge of the hood with right sides facing. Sew them together, then trim the seam allowance to ⅛" (0.3cm). Overlock the raw edge of the hood front, then fold it over to cover the trimmed seam allowance. From the right side of the fabric, sew it in place by stitching in the ditch of the previous seam.

Stitch the neck seam.

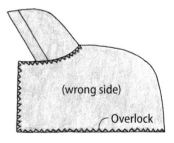

(wrong side)

Overlock

6 **Join the body and hood pieces.** Align the neck seam of the hood with that of the body with right sides facing. Match up the center seams, pin the layers in place, then sew them together.

7 **Overlock the edges.**
Beginning from the neck seam through the center front to the hem, overlock all the raw edges.

8 **Stitch the center front of the body piece.**
Align the center front seams of the body piece, sew them together, then press the seam open. Top stitch two seams ¼" (0.5cm) to the left and right of the finished seam.

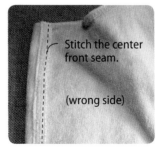

Stitch the center front seam.

(wrong side)

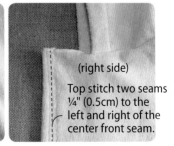

(right side)

Top stitch two seams ¼" (0.5cm) to the left and right of the center front seam.

9 **Stitch the neckline.** Fold under and press the seam allowance at the center front of the body and the seam allowance around the neckline. Turn the robe right side out and top stitch the fold in place.

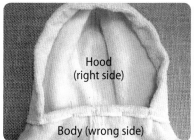

Hood (right side)

Body (wrong side)

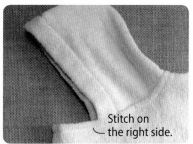

Stitch on the right side.

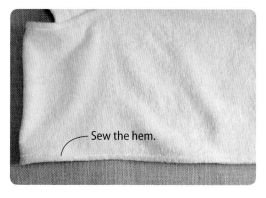

Sew the hem.

10 **Sew the hem.** Fold under the hem by ⅜" (1cm), and, similar to step 9, turn the robe right side out and sew the fold in place from the right side. There is no need to make back stitches; simply overlap your beginning stitches by about ⅜" (1cm).

11 **Decorate with embroidery.** Embroider patterns of hens and chicks on the body and the hood for decoration.

 ## Help at bath time

Bath Towels

This is an essential towel set for bathing your dog or for traveling with him! Super-soft, double-sided terrycloth is perfect for this project. Make two towels, one large and one small. You can also embroider your dog's name on the towels.

Mommy, is today the day for my bubble bath?

Bath Towels

SIZES : Body towel 29½" x 25⅝" (75 x 65cm)
Foot towel 10⅝" x 9⅞" (27 x 25cm)

FABRIC : ¾ yd. (¾m) of 100% cotton double-sided
terrycloth (⅛" [0.4cm] loop length)

NOTIONS : Two decorative fabric labels
Bias tape: 3¼ yds. (3¼m) for body towel,
1¼ yds. (1¼m) for foot towel
Water-soluble fabric glue

1 **Cut the fabric pattern pieces out.** Cut the rectangles from your fabric for each towel: 29½" x 25⅝" (75 x 65cm) for the body towel, 10⅝" x 9⅞" (27 x 25cm) for the foot towel. There is no need to add seam allowances, as the edges will be bound by bias tape.

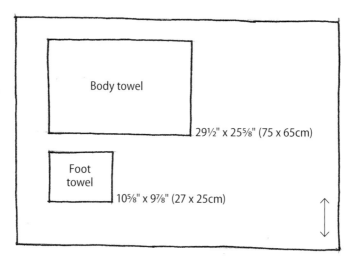

Body towel

29½" x 25⅝" (75 x 65cm)

Foot towel

10⅝" x 9⅞" (27 x 25cm)

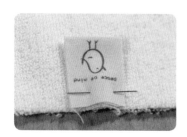

Slightly pull on the bias tape and stick it to the terrycloth.

2 **Secure the fabric labels.** Pin the fabric labels to the bottom right corner of the towel pieces.

3 **Secure the bias tape, part 1.** Choose a starting point for your bias tape (avoid corners), and dab the fabric glue on the tape to stick it to the terrycloth edges.

4 **Secure the bias tape, part 2.**
When reaching the corner, tuck the bias tape inward to create a triangle shape, then secure the folds with more fabric glue. When you reach the beginning, fold under the end of the tape and glue it to cover the beginning.

Fold in the bias tape here to create a mitered corner.

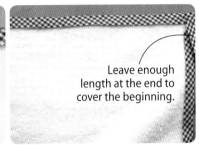

Leave enough length at the end to cover the beginning.

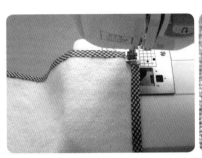

Back stitch 2–3 times at the corners.

5 **Sew the bias tape.**
Stitch the bias tape in place all around four edges. Back stitch diagonally 2–3 times at the corners to reinforce the strength of the corners.

While sewing the terrycloth, there will be a fair amount of fiber shedding. Prepare a mini vacuum to use while you sew.

Two cute tops

Twin Shirt Set

If there are two or more dogs in your family, you shouldn't miss the fun of dressing them in matching clothes. Let's make a casual T-shirt and a girly shirt with the same fabric!

Hey! Are we wearing the same clothes?

♥The girly shirt with a cute flounced bottom lightly swaying with the wind

Mommy!
Are you calling me?

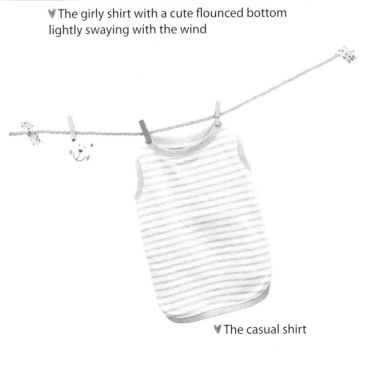

♥The casual shirt

Twin Shirt Set

SIZES	XS through XL
FABRIC	⅓–½ yd. (⅓–½m) of striped cotton interlock
NOTIONS	⅛ yd. (⅛m) of ribbed knit fabric for binding

Making the Flounced Shirt

1 **Cut the fabric pattern pieces out.** Lay the pattern pieces on the wrong side of the fabric and trace the pattern. Add a ⅜" (1cm) seam allowance for all edges except for the hem of the skirt, which needs ¾" (2cm). Cut the fabric pieces out. Cut your rib binding strips following the tip found on page 62.

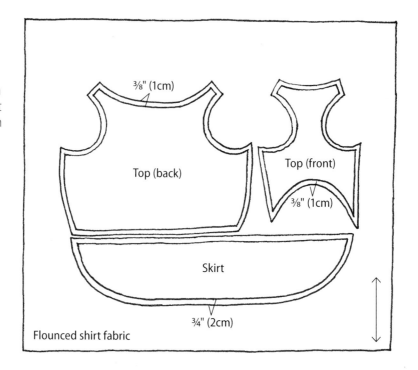

⅜" (1cm)

Top (back)

Top (front)

⅜" (1cm)

Skirt

¾" (2cm)

Flounced shirt fabric

2 **Stitch the shoulder and side seams.** Align the shoulder seams of the top front and back pieces together with right sides facing. Pin, then stitch the shoulders in place. Do the same for the side seams, aligning and pinning the stripe pattern first. Overlock the seam allowances.

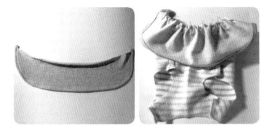

3 **Make the flounced skirt—gather the fabric.** Make a double-fold hem on the bottom of the skirt by folding the fabric over by ⅜" (1cm) twice and stitching it in place. Sew a running stitch ¼" (0.5cm) from the waistline edge to gather the fabric until it is the length of the top back bottom edge. Align the center of the skirt with the center of the top back, then line up the rest of the raw edges. With the gathers even and pinned, sew the layers together.

4 **Make the flounced skirt—fold the seam allowance.** Overlock the seam allowance at the waistline. Fold in the bottom edge of the inside front and sew the fold in place.

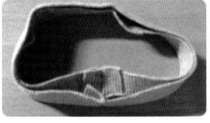

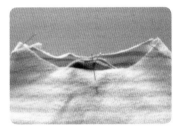

5 **Make the rib bindings.** From the rib binding strips (1 for collar, 2 for armholes), fold them in half to line up the short ends with right sides together, and sew the short edges with a ⅜" (1cm) seam allowance. Press the seams open, then fold the strip in half lengthwise with wrong sides together and press them flat. This should result in three fabric rings.

6 **Mark the positions of the rib bindings on the garment.** Fold the rib binding in half at the seam to find the half point. Then bring the half points together to find and mark the quarter points.

7 **Attach the rib bindings.** The length of the collar rib binding is shorter than the collar circumference, so stretch it slightly as you pin it around the collar to match up the marked points. Sew the rib binding around the collar edge with right sides together. Overlock the seam allowance, then press the seam toward the dress body. Edge stitch the seam allowance to the dress body. Repeat this procedure with the armhole binding.

Making the Casual Shirt

1 **Cut the fabric pattern pieces out.** Lay the pattern pieces on the wrong side of the fabric and trace the pattern. Add a ⅜" (1cm) seam allowance, then cut the fabric pieces out.

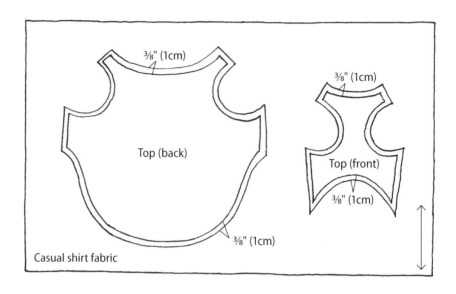

⅜" (1cm)

Top (back)

⅜" (1cm)

Top (front)

⅜" (1cm)

⅜" (1cm)

Casual shirt fabric

2 **Stitch the shoulder and side seams.** Align the shoulder seams from the top front and back with right sides facing, then sew the edges together. Overlock the seam allowances, then repeat this with the side seams as well.

3 **Make the rib bindings.** From the rib binding strips (1 for collar, 2 for armholes, 1 for hem), fold them in half to line up the short ends with right sides together, and sew the short edges with a ⅜" (1cm) seam allowance. Press the seams open, then fold the strip in half lengthwise with wrong sides together and press them flat. This should result in four fabric rings. Refer to steps 6 and 7 for the flounced shirt to attach the rib binding to the collar, armholes, and hem.

Calculating the length of the rib bindings

You can purchase commercially available rib binding and bias tape, but you can also make your own from the garment fabric. Cut strips from the crosswise (stretchiest) grain of knit fabrics or from the bias of woven fabrics. Measure the opening you wish to bind, such as the hem: say 20" (51cm). Take 80% of this number (90% for woven fabrics), then add the seam allowances (⅜" [1cm] for each side): 16" + ¾" = 16¾" (41 + 2 = 43cm). Therefore, you should cut a 16¾" (43cm) strip to fit the hem circumference.

Stylish in the cold

Leopard Cape and Stole

In the bone-chilling winds of winter, it is very important to keep your dog warm. When taking him out, putting a simple outer garment on him can help keep him warm. A fancy leopard print cape and stole are also practical items to protect your dog from the cold weather.

Stole

Cape

❤ You can choose one of them to make, or make both!

Leopard Cape and Stole

SIZES	XS through XL
FABRIC	¼–⅓ yd. (¼–⅓m) of fleece fabric for outer cape/stole ¼–⅓ yd. (¼–⅓m) of silky twill fabric for lining
NOTIONS	Pair of hook and eye closures Decorative buttons 1 yd. of black leather cording Batting for pom-poms

Making the Cape

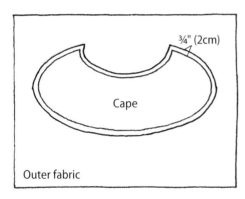

¾" (2cm)

Cape

Outer fabric

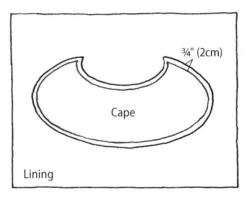

¾" (2cm)

Cape

Lining

1 **Cut the fabric pattern pieces out.** Lay the pattern pieces on the wrong side of the fabric and trace the pattern. Add a ¾" (2cm) seam allowance, then cut the fabric pieces out. Because the fabric used in this project is a pile fabric, a wider seam allowance than usual is used. To prevent excessive shedding of the pile fabric while cutting, overlock the fabric edges in advance.

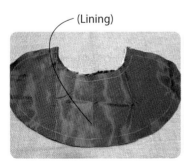

(Lining)

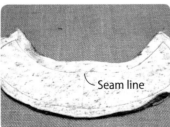

Seam line

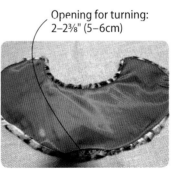

Opening for turning: 2–2⅜" (5–6cm)

2 **Join the outer fabric and lining.** Layer the cape outer fabric and lining pieces with right sides facing and sew them together around the perimeter, but leave a 2–2⅜" (5–6cm) opening for turning. Trim and notch the seam allowances, then turn the cape right side out through the opening.

3 **Sew the lining.** Close the opening in the previous step with blind stitches. Spread out the cape with the lining facing up, and roll the seam so the outer fabric peeks out from beneath the lining. Sew the lining in place with a running stitch so it stays this way.

4 **Attach the hook and the eye.** Attach the hook and the eye on each inside upper corner of the cape.

5 **Finish.** Attach the decorative buttons on the upper corners of the right side of the cape.

Making the Stole

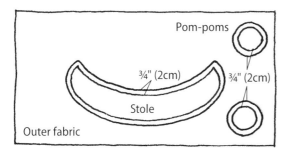

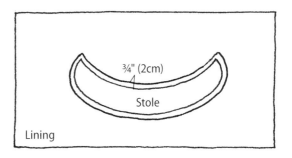

1 **Cut the fabric pattern pieces out.** Lay the pattern pieces on the wrong side of the fabric and trace the pattern. Add a ¾" (2cm) seam allowance, then cut the fabric pieces out. Because the fabric used in this project is a pile fabric, a larger than usual seam allowance is used.

2 **Make the stole.** Follow the steps for making the cape in order to make the stole.

3 **Make the pom-poms.** Take the pom-pom pieces and sew a running stitch around the perimeter. Pull at the thread to gather it up, then fill it with batting before it's completely closed. Finish the pom-poms with hand stitching, then hand sew them to the ends of the leather cords.

4 **Attach the leather strings.** Hand stitch the leather cords to the ends of the stole.

very cozy T-shirt

Sporty and convenient

T-Shirt

A simple T-shirt is the best leisurewear at home. This one is made of cotton. Since the fabric is stretchable, be sure to relax the size of neck and armholes to make it more comfortable for your dog.

T-Shirt

SIZES	XS through XL
FABRIC	⅓–½ yd. (⅓–½m) of cartoon printed cotton interlock
	½–⅔ yd. (½–⅔m) of blue single knit jersey for bias binding
NOTIONS	Two decorative buttons
	10" x 10" (25 x 25cm) square of lightweight fusible interfacing

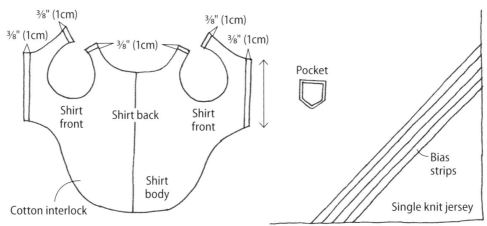

1 **Cut the fabric pattern pieces out.** Lay the pattern pieces on the wrong side of the fabric and trace the pattern. Add a ⅜" (1cm) seam allowance at the shoulder and center front seams as well as the pocket. Cut bias strips from the jersey to bind the neck, armholes, and hem; see the tip on page 72 for instructions on the strip lengths.

Carefully cut and press the corners to prevent the seam allowance from being bulky.

Overlocked edges

Fold in the seam allowance and press.

2 **Make the pocket.** Iron the fusible interfacing to the back of the pocket piece. Finish all the raw edges by overlocking the edges. Fold in the seam allowance along the side and bottom edges, but leave the top of the pocket unfolded.

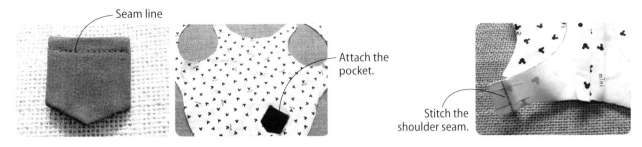

Seam line

Attach the pocket.

Stitch the shoulder seam.

3 **Attach the pocket.** Fold under the ⅜" (1cm) seam allowance at the top of the pocket, then sew it in place. Using water-soluble fabric glue or fusible web, apply the pocket to the front of the garment. Edge stitch it in place along the sides and bottom, leaving the top edge open.

4 **Stitch the shoulder seam.** Line up the shoulder straps with right sides facing and sew the shoulder seam. Finish the seams by overlocking the edges, then press the seams open.

Overlock the seam allowances then press the seams open.

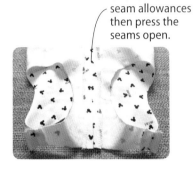

Bias tape

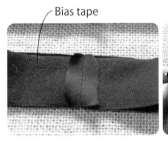

5 **Sew the center front.** Fold the shirt body in half, aligning the raw edges of the center front from the right and left sides. Sew them together with right sides facing, then overlock the seam allowances and press them open.

6 **Make the neck binding.** Layer the short ends of the neck binding together with right sides facing and sew them with a ⅜" (1cm) seam allowance. Press the seam allowance open, then fold the binding in half to find the halfway point. Mark both with pins.

7 **Attach the neck binding, part 1.** Mark the center of the neckline of the shirt body the same way as the bias binding. Align the center of the binding with that of the neck with right sides facing, and sew the binding around the neckline with a ¼" (0.7cm) seam allowance. Pull lightly at the jersey while you sew to make it fit around the opening.

8 **Attach the neck binding, part 2.** Press the binding away from the neckline, then fold under the raw edge by ¼" (0.7cm). Fold the binding in half so that the folded edge of the binding just covers the seam line from the previous step. Sew this fold in place, then press it so the stretched fabric and stitches shrink back and the end result looks more finished.

Seam line

Pull the binding with an even strength as you sew.

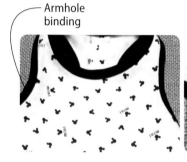

Armhole binding

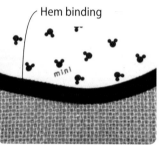

Hem binding

9 **Bind armholes and hem.** Bind the armholes and hem the same way as the neck was bound.

10 **Attach decorative buttons.** After ironing the armholes and hem, attach the decorative buttons to the pocket.

Measuring the length of bias tape
Measure the length of each part of the shirt with a tape measure, then find the length of bias tape you need using the following method. Use a width of 1⅜" (3.5cm) while cutting.
Length of neck binding = neck circumference − ¾" (2cm) + ¾" (2cm) (for seam allowance)
Length of armhole binding = armhole length − ⅜" (1cm) + ¾" (2cm) (for seam allowance)
Length of hem binding = hem length − ⅜" (1cm) + ¾" (2cm) (for seam allowance)

Cute play outfit

Apron and Bandana

In this adorable apron and bandana, your dog looks like he is ready to whip up something tasty in the kitchen! You'll be the one who has to feed him, though.

What shall we do today?

It's time to play~

Apron and Bandana

SIZES : XS through XL

FABRIC : ½–⅔ yd. (½–⅔m) of brown polka-dot linen
for outer fabric
¼–½ yd. (¼–½m) of 100% cotton for lining

NOTIONS : 40–46" (102–117cm) of ⅜" (1cm) wide lace
Three buttons, ⅜" (1cm) wide
Five invisible snaps
⅛ yd. (⅛m) of lightweight fusible interfacing
Stay tape

Making the Apron

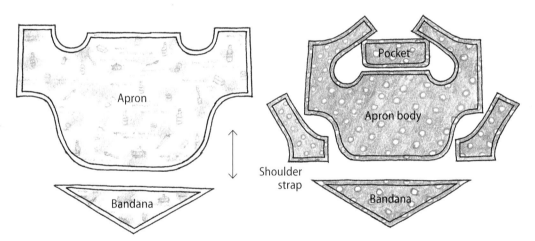

1
Cut the fabric pattern pieces out. Lay the pattern pieces on the wrong side of the fabric and trace the pattern with a ⅜" (1cm) seam allowance. Cut out the fabric pieces. You should have one outer fabric piece and one lining piece for the body, two outer fabric pieces for shoulder straps (polka-dot linen), one outer fabric piece for the pocket (polka-dot linen), and one outer fabric and lining piece for the bandana. Note that the shoulder strap pattern is traced from the apron body pattern.

2
Sew the outer fabric body piece and shoulder straps together. Layer the outer fabric body piece and shoulder strap pieces with right sides together and sew them along the shoulder seam. Press the seam allowances open, and pin the decorative lace on top of the finished seams. Edge stitch the lace in place.

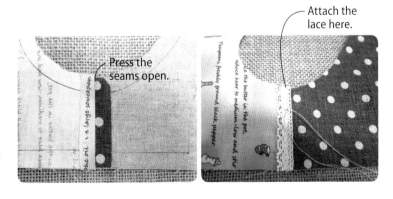

Press the seams open.

Attach the lace here.

3 **Make the pocket.** Finish all four raw edges of the pocket piece. Fold under each edge by ⅜" (1cm) and press them in place. Sew a straight seam down the center for decoration, then cut a length of the narrow lace, fold the two ends in, and edge stitch it to the top edge of the pocket.

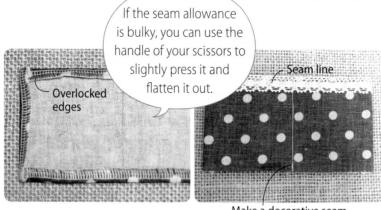

If the seam allowance is bulky, you can use the handle of your scissors to slightly press it and flatten it out.

Overlocked edges

Seam line

Make a decorative seam down the center.

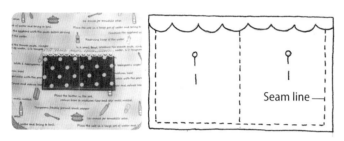

Seam line

4 **Attach the pocket.** Align the center of the pocket with the center of the outer apron body to determine the pocket position. Pin the pocket in place, or use fabric adhesive. Edge stitch the pocket in place around the sides and bottom.

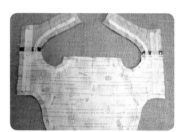

5 **Stick the fusible interlining and interlining tape together.** Cut the fusible interfacing into ⅝" (1.5cm) strips and iron them to the left and right edges of the body piece on the wrong side of the fabric. This is the placket part of the apron where the invisible snaps will be installed. Iron the stay tape around the armholes.

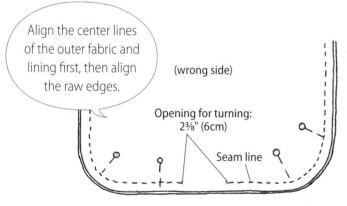

Align the center lines of the outer fabric and lining first, then align the raw edges.

(wrong side)

Opening for turning: 2⅜" (6cm)

Seam line

6 **Join the outer fabric and lining.** Align the outer fabric and lining with right sides facing and leave a 2⅜" (6cm) opening for turning at the hem. Match up the edges and pin the layers in place. Sew along the edges, skipping the opening for turning. Back tack several times at the start and end of the seam to secure it. Trim the seam allowance to ¼" (0.5cm).

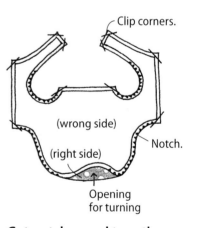

Clip corners.

(wrong side)

(right side)

Notch.

Opening for turning

7 **Cut notches and turn the apron right side out.** Clip the corners and cut the notches at the curves of the seam allowance. Turn the apron right side out, starting from the shoulder and going through the opening at the hem. Adjust the seams of the garment and iron it flat.

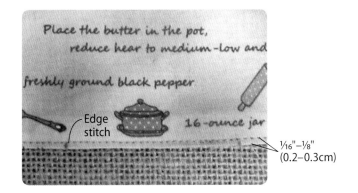

Sew the straps to the garment.

8 **Sew edge stitches along the finished seam.** Sew an edge stitch just outside the finished seam ¹⁄₁₆"–⅛" (0.2–0.3cm) from the edge.

9 **Attach the buttons.** Attach the invisible snaps where the pattern markings indicate. Fold the straps over and mark their positions on the back of the garment, then sew the straps and wooden buttons in place.

Making the Bandana

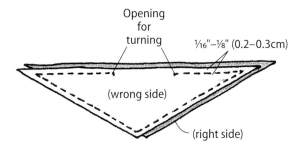

Opening for turning

¹⁄₁₆"–⅛" (0.2–0.3cm)

(wrong side)

(right side)

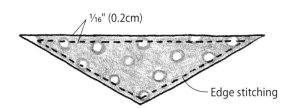

¹⁄₁₆" (0.2cm)

Edge stitching

1 **Join the outer fabric and lining.** Layer the outer fabric and lining fabric with right sides facing, then sew them together along the edges. Leave a 2–2⅜" (5–6cm) opening for turning. After sewing, trim the seam allowance to ¼" (0.5cm).

2 **Sew the edge stitching.** Turn the bandana right side out through the opening for turning. Edge stitch around the perimeter of the bandana, ¹⁄₁₆" (0.2cm) from the edge.

3 **Attach the lace and buttons.** Center the remaining narrow lace along the long edge of the bandana. Pin it in place, then edge stitch the lace onto the bandana. Attach the wooden button at the tip of the bandana.

Suitable for every dog

Plaid Dress

This red plaid dress is a never-go-wrong item suitable for every dog. It makes your dog look fresh and full of spirit. You can make barrettes or hair ties with the same fabric to match the dress.

♥ Attach cute buttons and bows to the back as decorations.

Plaid Dress

SIZES	XS through XL
FABRIC	½–⅔ yd. (½–⅔m) of cotton/linen blend fabric for outer dress and lining
NOTIONS	⅛ yd. (⅛m) of lightweight fusible interfacing Three decorative buttons Invisible snaps Stay tape 1¾–2¾ yd. (1¾–2¾m) of narrow decorative lace Red beads Pin base

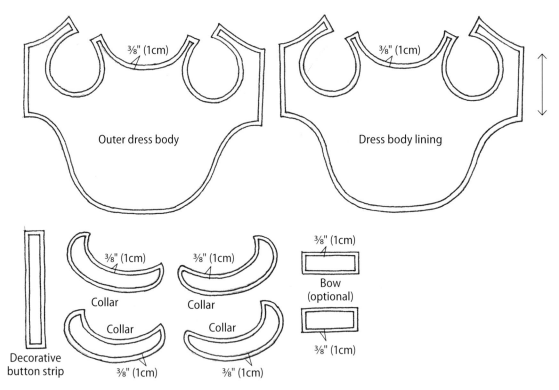

Outer dress body

Dress body lining

⅜" (1cm)

Collar

Collar

Collar

Collar

Decorative button strip

Bow (optional)

⅜" (1cm)

1 **Cut the fabric pattern pieces out.** Lay the pattern pieces on the wrong side of the fabric and trace the pattern. Add a ⅜" (1cm) seam allowance, then cut the fabric pieces out. Also cut two additional collar pieces and one button strip piece from the interfacing. Iron the fusible interfacing to the wrong side of the outer collar pieces and the decorative button strip. Iron stay tape to the neck and arm holes as well as the center front edges of the dress (button plackets).

2 **Make the decorative button strip, part 1.** Fold under the short edges of the button strip by ⅜" (1cm), then sew the folds in place. Line up the lace, with the scalloped edges pointing towards the middle of the strip, ¼" (0.7cm) inside the long raw edges of the strip. Sew them in place along the straight edges of the lace.

 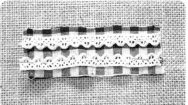

3 **Make the decorative button strip, part 2.** Fold under the long edges of the strip by ⅜" (1cm) and press them flat. The scalloped edge of the lace should peek out just behind the strip; trim the seam allowance to reduce bulk. Fold under the short edges of the strip by ⅜" (1cm) once more and press it flat.

Seam allowance at the end

If the seam allowance is bulky, use the handle of your scissors to press it thinner.

After cutting the fabric pieces, remember to mark the front and back on the collar pieces to prevent mixing them up.

  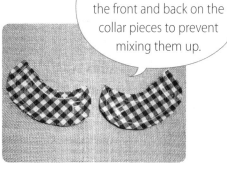

4 **Make the collar, part 1.** Layer the lace strip along the rounded edge of the outer collar piece with right sides facing, the bottom edge aligned ¼" (0.5cm) above the raw edge. Layer the collar lining on top, then sew the pieces together, leaving the neck edge open for turning right side out. Repeat this with the other collar pieces, resulting in a right and left collar piece.

5 **Make the collar, part 2.** Trim the seam allowance to ⅛" (0.3cm), and cut notches at the curves. Turn the collar right side out and iron it flat, then edge stitch along the finished seam.

6 **Stitch the shoulder lines.** Align the shoulder seams of the outer dress and sew them together; press the seams open. Repeat this with the dress lining as well.

7 **Sew the decorative button strip.** Line up the decorative button strip made in step 3 at the center of the outer dress front, and pin it in place. Edge stitch it in place, but be careful, as the strip is much thicker than the dress. Take care so that the finished product looks professional.

8 **Join the collar and outer dress pieces.** Pin the two collar pieces on the left and right sides of the center back of the outer dress, making sure each collar piece is on the correct side. Sew them in place with a ¼" (0.5cm) seam allowance, either by machine or by hand.

9 **Join the outer dress and lining, part 1.** Align the lace strip along the hem similarly to the previous steps, then secure it in place with pins or basting stitches. Layer the lining on top, then sew it in place around the raw edges (except the armholes). Be sure to leave a 2¾"–3⅛" (7–8cm) opening for turning the dress right side out. After sewing, trim the seam allowance to ¼" (0.5cm). Cut notches on the curves, then turn the dress right side out.

10 **Join the outer dress and lining, part 2.** For the bulky seam allowances, you can trim them or press them with the handle of your scissors. However, for the neckline, you need to open up the seam and under stitch the seam allowance to the lining of the dress, 1/16" (0.1cm) away from the seam, to make the collar lay flat. Open up the armholes in the dress to do this.

11 **Complete the armholes.** Line up the raw armhole edges of the outer dress and lining and overlock them together. Line up the lace over the armholes with the bottom edge of the lace covering the overlock stitches and the ends overlapping at the bottom of the armhole. Baste the lace in place, then fold under the armhole by 3/8" (1cm) and edge stitch the fold in place 1/16" (0.2cm) from the fold.

12 **Attach buttons and a bow.** Edge stitch along the edges of the dress, except for the armholes. Attach buttons along the decorative button strip and the invisible snaps along the dress placket. Buy or make a decorative bow and sew the red beads on the center. Using hot glue, glue the bow to a pin base, then pin the bow to the bottom of the decorative strip.

Lovely and energetic

Knitted Cape

This is a very adorable hand-knitted cape. It is very easy to make and is also easy to put on and to take off. You can enhance your finished product by adding some little flowers on the cape as decorations to make it more charming.

❦ Crochet some little flowers on the cape as decorations.

❦ You can also make barrettes with the crocheted flowers!

Knitted Cape

SIZE | Neck circumference 10⅝" (27cm),
chest circumference 16⅝" (42cm)

TOOLS AND | Size 4 (3.5mm) knitting needles
MATERIALS | Size G (4mm) crochet hook
Light worsted yarn
Ribbon
Yarn needle

KNITTING GAUGE | 1" = 5 stitches x 7.5 rows
(1cm = 2.5 stitches x 3 rows)

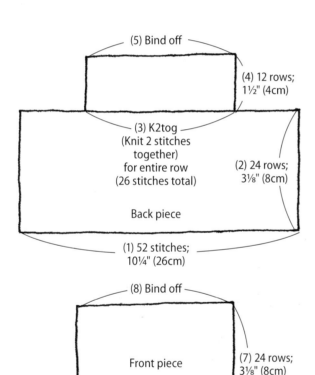

(5) Bind off

(4) 12 rows;
1½" (4cm)

(3) K2tog
(Knit 2 stitches
together)
for entire row
(26 stitches total)

(2) 24 rows;
3⅛" (8cm)

Back piece

(1) 52 stitches;
10¼" (26cm)

(8) Bind off

Front piece

(7) 24 rows;
3⅛" (8cm)

(6) 26 stitches;
5⅛" (13cm)

 1 **Knit the back piece.** With the size 4 (3.5mm) needle, cast on 52 stitches (10¼" [26cm] long). Knit in stockinette stitch for 24 rows (3⅛" [8cm]). For the next row, k2tog (knit 2 together) for the entire row, 26 stitches total. Continue in stockinette stitch for 12 rows (1½" [4cm]), then bind off.

 2 **Knit the front piece.** With the size 4 (3.5mm) needle, cast on 26 stitches (5⅛" [13cm] long). Knit in stockinette stitch for 24 rows (3⅛" [8cm]), then bind off.

 3 **Join the front and back pieces.** Sew the front to the back with leftover yarn and the yarn needle. Add trim to the bottom of the cape by crocheting slip stitches around the bottom edge for one round. Then crochet with an edging pattern of your choice, such as a simple decorative edge: chain 2 stitches, skip 1 stitch, 1 single crochet, then repeat for the entire round.

 4 **Decorate.** Crochet some flowers on the cape, or buy some knitted decorative items. Use hot glue to apply the flowers or hairpins to make a matching set with the cape.

The handiest winter item

Hat with Scarf

This is such a beautiful knitted set! After putting on his hat and scarf, your dog looks so adorable. These are the most eye-catching winter accessories, perfect to wear during a walk in winter.

I am the star of the winter! I love running in the snow!

Hmm, your hat is the same as mine. It seems that you also have good taste.

My mom made this for me.

Hat with Scarf

SIZE : Head circumference (horizontal) 9⅞" (25cm);
head circumference (vertical) 2¾" (7cm)

TOOLS AND
MATERIALS :
Size 2 (3mm) knitting needles
Size G (4mm) crochet needle
Sport weight yarn in peach, pink, white, and blue
Yarn needle
Pom-poms
Invisible thread

KNITTING GAUGE : 1" = 6.5 stitches x 7.5 rows
(1cm = 2.5 stitches x 3 rows)

Make the Hat

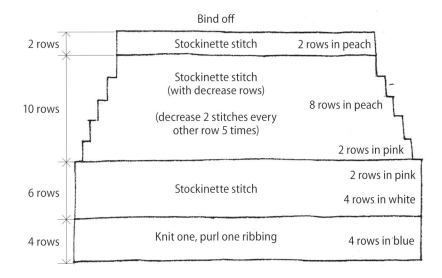

Bind off

2 rows	Stockinette stitch	2 rows in peach
10 rows	Stockinette stitch (with decrease rows) (decrease 2 stitches every other row 5 times)	8 rows in peach
		2 rows in pink
6 rows	Stockinette stitch	2 rows in pink / 4 rows in white
4 rows	Knit one, purl one ribbing	4 rows in blue

1 **Calculate the stitch count for the front piece.**
Calculate the stitch count you need to create the hat. To create the finished size shown, 9⅞" x 2¾" (25 x 7cm), the front half should be 5" x 2¾" (12.5 x 7cm). Divide this by the number of stitches per inch you achieved in your knitted gauge swatch. For this example you would need 32 stitches by 21 rows (5" x 6.5 sts/in = 32 sts; 2¾" x 7.5 rows/in = 21 rows) (12.5cm x 2.5 sts/cm = 32 sts; 7cm x 3 rows/cm = 21 rows).

2 **Knit the front piece.** With the starting number, 32 stitches, calculated, cast on 32 stitches and knit with a knit 1, purl 1 ribbing for 4 rows in blue. Knit stockinette stitch for 4 rows in white. Switch to pink and knit stockinette stitch for 2 more rows.

Tips
• Knit the hat and scarf separately then sew them together.
• When knitting the hat, knit the front and back pieces separately then sew them together.
• Adjust the length of the scarf to your needs.
• To keep the hat from falling off your dog's head, you can sew an elastic strap on the bottom. You can also crochet an additional string of chain stitches as the hat strap.

3 **Decrease rows.** Next are the decrease rows. Decrease 1 stitch at the beginning and end of the next row (2 stitches total), then continue in stockinette stitch for the following row. Switch to the peach color, then repeat the decrease row 4 more times for every other row—decreasing 10 stitches total. Continue in plain stockinette stitch for 2 more rows and bind off. Note that this makes 22 rows total, to make the colored stripes even.

4 **Knit the back piece.** Knit up the back of the hat the same as the front. After binding off, leave a 4"–6" (10–15cm) long thread tail.

5 **Finish.** Align the front and the back pieces of the hat, and thread the yarn needle with the long thread tail. Pull at your last binding stitches to even them out if necessary. Run the needle through the stitches of the last row and pull at the yarn to gather it up so it fits the crown of your dog's head.

6 **Join the front and back hat pieces.** Stitch the front of the hat to the back, leaving an opening on each side for the dog's ears.

7 **Attach the pom-pom.** Make or use a purchased pom-pom for the top of the hat. Trim it to a round shape, then sew it to the top of the hat.

Make the Scarf

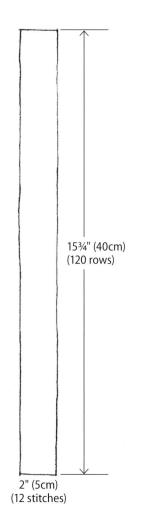

15¾" (40cm)
(120 rows)

2" (5cm)
(12 stitches)

1 **Knit the scarf.** Cast on 12 stitches and knit with a knit 1, purl 1 rib for as many rows as you prefer; done here were 120 rows (2" x 15¾" [5 x 40cm]). Switch out colors for the stripes whenever you prefer as well.

2 **Join the scarf and the hat.** After knitting the scarf, align the center edge of the scarf to the bottom edge of the back of the hat, and sew it in place with the yarn needle.

3 **Attach the pom-poms.** Make or use several purchased multicolored pom-poms for the scarf trim. Attach them with short crocheted chain stitches to the edge of the scarf.

4 **Finish.** Iron the hat with the scarf—the end result will look more finished and be stretchier.

🐑 Dress up for any occasion

Button-Down Shirt

With this plaid shirt, you dog looks like a model student when sitting quietly. Or you can transform him into a charming gentleman by putting a bow tie around his neck.

♥ The back of the shirt is even more elegant.

Button-Down Shirt

SIZES	XS through XL
FABRIC	⅓–⅔ yd. (⅓–⅔m) of plaid cotton
NOTIONS	Invisible or pearl snaps ¼ yd. (¼m) of lightweight fusible interfacing

1 **Cut the fabric pattern pieces out.** Lay the pattern pieces on the wrong side of the fabric and trace around the pieces, adding a ⅜" (1cm) seam allowance, except for the hems, which require a ¾" (2cm) seam allowance. Cut out the fabric, then cut two collar pieces from the fusible interfacing. Iron the interfacing to the wrong side of the collar pieces.

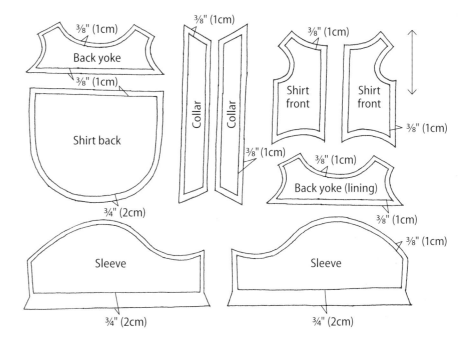

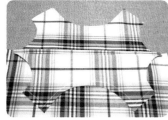

2 **Join the back to the back yoke pieces.** Layer the straight edge of the shirt back between the two yoke pieces with right sides facing. Sew the three layers together, then press the seam allowance toward the back yoke. Edge stitch the previous seam.

3 **Interface the placket front.** Cut strips of interfacing wide enough to cover the shirt plackets found along the center front of the shirt front pieces. Iron the fusible interfacing to the wrong side of the placket.

Join the front and back pieces at the shoulder.
Turn under the shoulder seams of the back yoke by ⅜" (1cm) and press them flat. Layer the shirt front shoulder seam between the two folded edges of the yoke and edge stitch them together.

Clip the seam allowance at the corners.

Edge stitching

Fold under ⁵⁄₁₆" (0.7cm) and press.

5 **Making the collar, part 1.** Line up the edges of the collar pieces together with right sides facing. Sew them together along the top and side edges, leaving the bottom open for the neck seam. Clip the seam allowances at the corners, and trim the seam allowances along the straight edges. Fold under one side of the bottom collar by ⁵⁄₁₆" (.7cm), which will be the inner collar for sewing the neck in step 8.

6 **Making the collar, part 2.** Turn the collar right side out and press it flat. Edge stitch the top and side edges.

7 **Sew the collar to the body.** Align the raw edge of the outer collar along the neck edge of the body of the shirt. Sew it in place, then grade and notch the finished seam allowance.

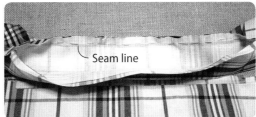

Seam line

Cut notches.

Pin in place.

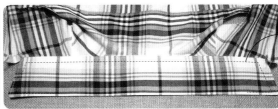

Sew 4 edges of the inner collar.

8 **Arrange the collar.** Lay the folded edge of the inner collar over the seam allowance and pin it in place. Sew along this folded edge, then topstitch along the perimeter of the collar.

9 **Sew the shirt sides.** Match up the side seams of the front and back pieces. Sew them together, finish the seam allowances, then press them toward the back of the shirt.

10 **Sewing the hem, part 1.** Hand sew a running stitch along the curved part of the back hem, leaving a long thread tail. Laying the pattern paper over the shirt back, pull the thread to gather the fabric along the shape of the pattern. Fold the hem once again, then pin and press it in place.

Shirt placket

While cutting, mark the front and back on the sleeve pieces to prevent from mixing them up.

11 **Sewing the hem, part 2.** Fold the front hem twice and pin it in place as well. Fold the shirt placket over and sew it in place.

12 **Make the sleeves.** Make a double fold hem at the cuff of both sleeves. Fold the sleeves in half lengthwise and sew them together along the side. Finish the seam allowances, then hand sew two lines of running stitches along the sleeve cap with long thread tails for easing the sleeves into the shirt body.

13 **Join the body and sleeves.** Line up the sleeve opening to the armhole of the shirt, matching up the side seams and pattern guidelines. Pull at the thread tails to ease the sleeve cap into the armhole with no puckering.

14 **Complete the sleeves and finish.** Finish the seam allowances from the sleeves. Attach the snaps to the placket front, or sew buttons and buttonholes as an alternative.

For a girly dog
Frilly Dress

This dress is made of beautiful printed pink linen with the quilted fabric pieces in matching colors. In this dress, your dog looks just like a princess.

If you have spare fabric, try to make some accessories with it, such as decorative fabric-covered buttons and barrettes.

lovely pink
linen dress

Frilly Dress

SIZES : XS through XL

FABRIC : ¼–⅓ yd. (¼–⅓m) of linen blend fabric for
outer dress
⅛–¼ yd. (⅛–¼m) of linen blend patchwork
fabric for contrast skirt
¼–½ yd. (¼–½m) of cotton for lining

NOTIONS : ⅛ yd. (⅛m) of lightweight fusible interfacing
Stay tape
Three fabric-covered buttons
Pearl snaps
⅔–1¼ yd. (⅔–1¼m) narrow decorative lace

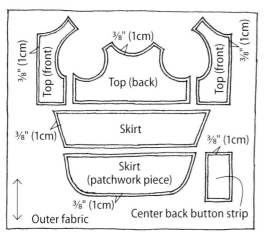

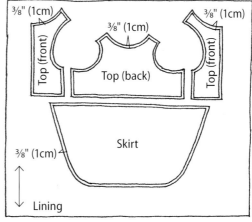

Outer fabric

- ⅜" (1cm) — Top (front)
- ⅜" (1cm) — Top (back)
- ⅜" (1cm) — Top (front)
- ⅜" (1cm) — Skirt
- Skirt (patchwork piece)
- ⅜" (1cm)
- ⅜" (1cm) — Center back button strip

Lining

- ⅜" (1cm) — Top (front)
- ⅜" (1cm) — Top (back)
- ⅜" (1cm) — Top (front)
- ⅜" (1cm) — Skirt

 Cut the fabric pattern pieces out. Lay the pattern pieces on the wrong side of the fabric and trace the pattern. Add a ⅜" seam allowance to all the edges, then cut the fabric pieces out. Also cut an additional button strip piece from the interfacing.

 Make the top—apply the fusible interfacing to the button strip. Mark the position of the center back button strip and lace on the outer dress top. To retain the garment's shape after washing, apply the fusible interfacing to the button strip. Fold under the long edges of the strip by ⅜" (1cm) and press them flat.

3 **Make the top—apply the lace to the button strip.** With the wrong side facing up, apply the lace (scalloped edge facing out) to the long edges of the button strip.

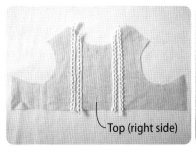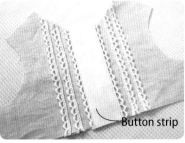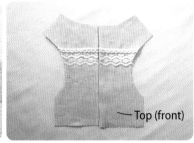

Top (right side)

Button strip

Top (front)

 Make the top—attach the lace to the top. Line up the lace strips along the pattern guidelines for the top (back) piece. Use a sewing awl to push it in place while sewing, if necessary. Trim the excess lace after sewing. Edge stitch the button strip in place as well on the top (back). Apply the lace along the top (front) as well.

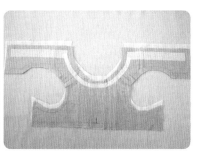

 Make the top—stitch the shoulder lines on the front and back pieces. Match up the shoulder seams on the front and back outer dress pieces and sew them together. Press the seams open when finished. Repeat this with the lining as well. Iron the stay tape along the neckline, center front seam (where the buttons will be attached), and armholes.

 Make the top—join the outer fabric and lining. Line up the top outer fabric and lining pieces with right sides facing and pin them together. Sew them together along the center front, neckline, and armholes, leaving the bottom and side straight edges free. Trim the seam allowances to ¼" (0.5cm), cut notches in the curves, turn the top right side out, and press it flat.

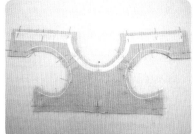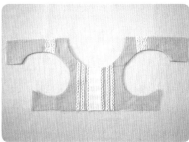

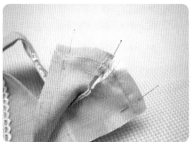

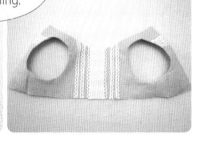

Align the seam allowances of the outer dress and lining.

7 **Make the top—stitch the side seams.** Align the side seams of the top, pin them in place, and stitch them together. After sewing, press the seam open. Fold the armhole back to how it was previously, then iron the seams in place.

8 **Make the skirt—join the outer fabric pieces.** Align the bottom edge of the outer skirt and the upper edge of the patchwork fabric with right sides facing. Sew them together, press the seam open, and apply the lace along the seam line.

9 **Make the skirt—join the outer fabric and lining.** Align the outer skirt and lining pieces, matching up the raw edges with right sides facing. Pin the fabric in place and sew around the sides and bottom. Trim the seam allowance to ¼" (0.5cm) and cut notches at the curves. Turn the skirt right side out, iron it flat, then edge stitch along the finished seam.

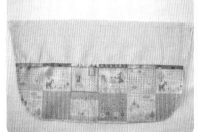

Sew edge stitches from the right side.

10 **Make the skirt—gather the fabric.** Loosen the thread tension and increase the stitch length of your machine, then sew a gathering stitch along the upper edge of the skirt. Leave a 4"–6" (10–15cm) thread tail after stitching, then pull on the thread to gather the fabric. If you are hand sewing, make two lines of running stitches, then pull on the threads to create gathers. Gather the fabric until it is as wide as the distance between the side seams. Knot the thread to secure the ruffles.

Join the top and the skirt, part 1. Match up the top outer fabric and the skirt with right sides facing. Align the center line and side seams, then pin and sew it in place. Be sure to only sew through the outer fabric and not the top lining.

 Join the top and the skirt, part 2. Fold under the seam allowance in the top lining, then sew it to the outer fabric with a blind stitch. Iron the seam, then edge stitch along the finished seam to make the join stronger.

 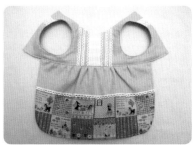

 Attach the buttons to finish. Sew the fabric-covered buttons to the center back button strip. Attach the decorative pearl snaps to the dress placket along the front seams to finish.

Here come the bride and groom

Bridal Gown and Tuxedo

Today is your dog's big day for walking down the aisle! Here are some special gifts: a beautiful bridal gown and a handsome tuxedo.

♥ A simple but gorgeous headdress

It's so beautiful from the back, too, isn't it?

Bridal Gown

SIZES	XS through XL
FABRIC	⅓–¾ yd. (⅓–¾m) of chiffon for outer dress
	⅓–¾ yd. (⅓–¾m) of white satin for lining
NOTIONS	2–3½ yds. (2–3½m) of ¾" (2cm) wide chiffon ribbon
	Decorative pearls
	Invisible thread
	Five invisible snaps

1 **Cut the fabric pattern pieces out.** Lay your pattern pieces on the wrong side of the fabric and trace the patterns. Do not add a seam allowance to the dress top; rather, simply cut a wide shape around the markings. Cut the top lining in a similar fashion. For the skirt, do add a ⅜" (1cm) seam allowance, and cut one from the outer fabric and one from the lining.

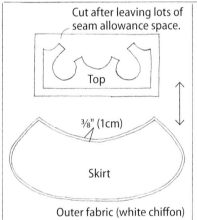

Cut after leaving lots of seam allowance space.

Top

⅜" (1cm)

Skirt

Outer fabric (white chiffon)

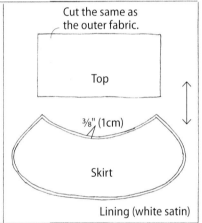

Cut the same as the outer fabric.

Top

⅜" (1cm)

Skirt

Lining (white satin)

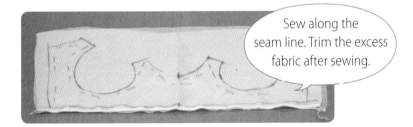

Sew along the seam line. Trim the excess fabric after sewing.

2 **Make the top—overlock the waistline.** Trim the bottom edges of the top outer fabric and lining to ⅜" (1cm) outside the traced line. Overlock the bottom raw edges of the outer fabric and lining separately. Layer the outer fabric and lining together with right sides facing, lining up the bottom edge, then pin the layers in place.

3 **Make the top—stitch the seam lines.** With the traced outline of the seam lines on the fabric, sew the lining to the outer fabric along the dress placket, collar, and armholes (leave the waistline and shoulder seams unsewn). From the dress placket, sew inward along the waist seam until the marked line indicated by the pattern, making an L shape.

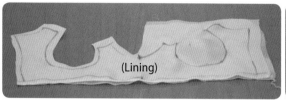

(Lining)

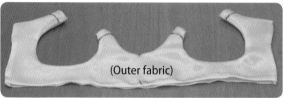

(Outer fabric)

4 **Make the top—trim the seam allowance and turn right side out.** Trim the seam allowances of the dress top to ¼" (0.5cm). Trim closer to ¹⁄₁₆" (0.2cm) at the armholes and collar. Cut notches in the curves, turn the top right side out, and iron it flat.

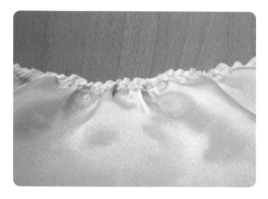

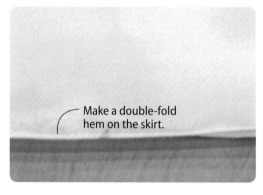

Make a double-fold hem on the skirt.

5 **Make the skirt—gather at the waistline.** Overlock the edges of the outer skirt fabric and lining. Sew two lines of running stitches along the waist of both skirt pieces (or, if using a sewing machine, lower the thread tension and lengthen the stitch), then pull the threads to gather the skirt to match the width of the dress top between the pattern markings.

6 **Make the skirt—sew the hem.** Sew a double-fold hem along the bottom edge of the skirt for both the outer fabric and lining. Layer the outer fabric and lining with both right sides facing up and pin them together.

7 **Join the top and skirt— stitch the waistline.** Align the waistline of the skirt with that of the dress top. Pin together the skirt with the outer fabric of the dress top only (with right sides facing) and sew them together with a ¹⁄₁₆" (0.2cm) seam allowance.

Align the skirt between the marked pattern guidelines of the dress top.

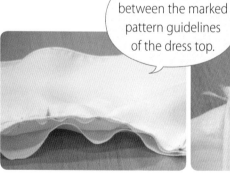

8 **Join the top and skirt—anchor the seam allowance and finish.** Fold under the seam allowance of the top lining, then use it to cover the previous seam. Sew the lining in place with blind stitches.

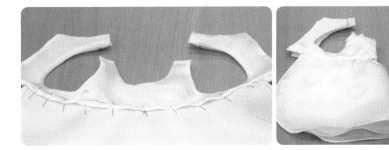

9 **Stitch the shoulder lines.** Fold under and tuck in the seam allowance at the shoulder seams of the top front, then press them in place. Take the shoulder seams from the top back, and tuck them into the opening from the top front, just enough to cover the seam allowance. Sew the layers in place with blind stitches. Attach the snap buttons to the placket front.

10 **Decorate the gown.** Gather the chiffon ribbon enough to cover the hem and placket edges, then sew them in place. Sew on the pearls with invisible thread. Also make waist and head accessories and glue them to pin bases and hairpins with hot glue.

Tuxedo

SIZES	XS through XL
FABRIC	½–⅔ yd. (½–⅔m) of black satin
	¼ yd. (¼m) of white satin
	⅛ yd. (⅛m) of yellow satin for bow tie
NOTIONS	⅔ yd. (⅔m) of ¼" (0.5cm) wide ribbon
	Three decorative gold buttons
	6" (15cm) of ¼" (0.5cm) wide gold silk string
	2" (5cm) patches of lightweight fusible interfacing

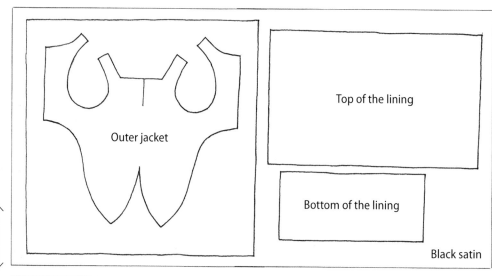

Outer jacket

Top of the lining

Bottom of the lining

Black satin

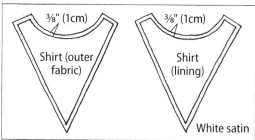

³⁄₈" (1cm)

Shirt (outer fabric)

³⁄₈" (1cm)

Shirt (lining)

White satin

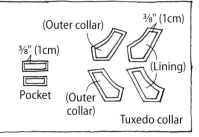

³⁄₈" (1cm)

³⁄₈" (1cm)

Bow tie

Yellow satin

³⁄₈" (1cm)

Pocket

(Outer collar)

³⁄₈" (1cm)

(Lining)

(Outer collar)

Tuxedo collar

Black satin

1 **Cut the fabric pattern pieces out.** Trace the outer tuxedo jacket pattern with no seam allowance; rather, cut generally around the pattern with lots of working space. Trace the lining in a similar fashion, but with a top and bottom section (as separated in the paper pattern). Trace the patterns for the shirt, collar, and bow tie—these do require a ³⁄₈" (1cm) seam allowance. Cut all the fabric pieces out.

Sew stay stitching (for reinforcement) at the corner of the collar and tuxedo tail. If there is not enough seam allowance added at these corners, there could be fraying when the coat is turned right side out. To prevent this, iron a patch of fusible interfacing to the outer coat first.

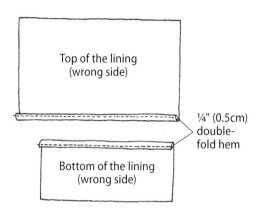

Top of the lining (wrong side)

¼" (0.5cm) double-fold hem

Bottom of the lining (wrong side)

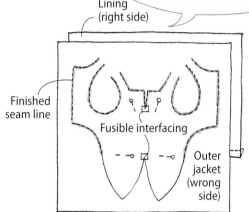

Lining (right side)

Finished seam line

Fusible interfacing

Outer jacket (wrong side)

2 **Make the lining.** Because the dog's tuxedo is so small that it is not easy to turn right side out after sewing together, the lining is split into a top and bottom and sewn separately. Fold under ¼" (0.5cm) twice along one edge of the top and bottom lining pieces, making a double-fold hem.

3 **Join the outer jacket and the top of the lining.** Align the outer jacket and the top lining pieces together with right sides facing. Pin the layers in place, then sew them together along the traced pattern lines for the placket front, front collar, front and back armholes, and back collar. Be sure not to sew the shoulder seams. Trim the seam allowances on the straight edges to ⅜" (1cm) and the curved edges to ¼" (0.5cm). Cut notches into the seam allowance on the curves.

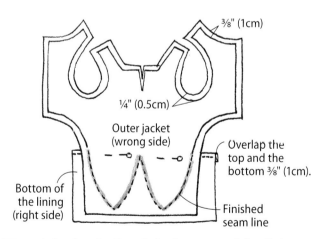

⅜" (1cm)

¼" (0.5cm)

Outer jacket (wrong side)

Overlap the top and the bottom ⅜" (1cm).

Bottom of the lining (right side)

Finished seam line

4 **Join the shell and the bottom of the lining.** Overlap the seam lines for the top and bottom lining by ⅜" (1cm), then pin the layers in place. Sew the bottom part of the jacket similarly to the top, stitching along the marked pattern lines.

5 **Turn the coat right side out and iron.** Trim the seam allowance to ¼" (0.5cm) and cut notches in the curves. Turn the jacket right side out and check for fraying or weakened corners at the collar and tail. Iron the jacket flat.

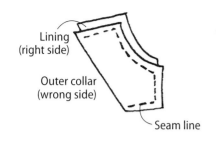

Lining
(right side)

Outer collar
(wrong side)

Seam line

6 **Make the collar.** Align the outer collar and the lining with right sides facing and sew the three sides (leaving the collar fold line open) as shown in the illustration. Trim the seam allowance to ⅛" (0.3cm). Turn the collar right side out and iron it flat, then repeat this with the other collar pieces.

7 **Attach the collar to the garment.** Align the two collar pieces in their positions on the garment. Pin and sew them in place. After the collar shape is adjusted, blind stitch the seam allowances on the lining side of the garment, out of view on the right side.

8 **Stitch the shoulder lines.** Pin the collar flat on the outer jacket back. Tuck in the seam allowances of the front and back shoulder seams and pin them in place. Stitch the shoulder seams together with blind stitches.

9 **Attach the decorative pocket.** Align the two pocket pieces together with right sides facing and sew them together along the two short edges and one long edge. Turn the pocket right side out and hand stitch it to the tuxedo. Tuck in three of the gold silk strings and secure them in parallel folds. Cut a piece of ribbon to bind the pocket, folding in the ends of the ribbon around the edges of the pocket, then sewing it in place with straight or blind stitches.

10 **Make the shirt, part 1.** Align the white satin shirt outer fabric and lining pieces together with right sides facing. Pin the layers in place, then sew them together along the collar line. After sewing, turn the seam allowance toward the lining and under stitch the seam allowance to the lining, ¹⁄₁₆" (0.2cm) from the seam. Trim the seam allowance to ⅛" (0.3cm).

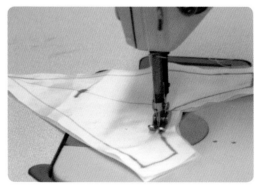

11 **Make the shirt, part 2.** Turn the shirt right side out and iron it flat. Sew the layers together along the seam line, then overlock the seam allowances.

12 **Make the bow tie.** Cut two pieces of yellow or red satin to create the bow tie: one 3½" x 2⅛" (9 x 5.5cm) and one 1½" x ⅜" (4 x 2cm). Fold the 2⅛" piece in half lengthwise and sew it along the long edge. Turn the tube right side out and sew a strip of decorative ribbon lengthwise along the middle. Fold the bow tie in half widthwise and stitch the raw ends together. Flatten the bow tie back out, with the center seam in the back, then run hand stitches through the middle to cinch up the bow and create the bow tie shape. Make the center of the bow tie similarly to the bow; wrap it around the bow and secure it in place with blind stitches.

13 **Join the tuxedo and the shirt.** Align the white satin shirt beneath the collar of the tuxedo jacket. Stitch it in place at the inner collar line, beneath the folded fabric so it is out of sight.

14 **Attach the bow tie.** Sew the bow tie to the center of the white satin shirt with overcast stitches.

15 **Attach buttons.** Attach three golden buttons at the front of the tuxedo jacket and the invisible snaps to the jacket placket to finish.

"Hanbok" for First Birthdays

Just like putting the prettiest Hanbok on a baby for their first birthday, you should dress your puppy up with the beautiful Hanbok to celebrate his first birthday. Don't forget to prepare their favorite snacks and toys at their birthday party!

♥ Cute accessories complete the traditional outfit

Hanbok is traditional Korean dress, currently worn for special occasions, including to celebrate an infant's first birthday. Enjoy making this special, vibrant piece of clothing for your puppy!

"Hanbok" for First Birthdays

Hanbok (traditional Korean celebratory dress) Outfit for Girls

Includes: saekdong jeogori (multicolored jacket), chima (skirt), and gulle (decorative headdress)

SIZES : XS through L

FABRIC : **Saekdong Jeogori (Multicolored Jacket):**
¼ yd. (¼m) of yellow Chinese silk
¼–⅓ yd. (¼–⅓m) of organza for lining
⅛ yd. (⅛m) of purple Chinese silk
⅛ yd. (⅛m) of white Chinese silk
⅛ yd. (⅛m) of green Chinese silk
⅛ yd. (⅛m) of blue Chinese silk
⅛ yd. (⅛m) of red Chinese silk
⅛ yd. (⅛m) of pink Chinese silk

Chima (Skirt):
¼ yd. (¼m) of cotton poplin
⅓–½ yd. (⅓–½m) of Chinese silk
    for outer skirt
⅓–½ yd. (⅓–½m) of Korean silk
    for padding
⅓–½ yd. (⅓–½m) of Korean chiffon
    with peach, pomegranate, and
    bergamot pattern for lining

FABRIC, *continued* : **Gulle (Decorative Headdress):**
⅛ yd. (⅛m) of red Chinese silk
⅛ yd. (⅛m) of yellow Chinese silk
⅛ yd. (⅛m) of green Chinese silk
⅛ yd. (⅛m) of purple Chinese silk
⅛ yd. (⅛m) of blue Chinese silk
⅛ yd. (⅛m) of white Chinese silk
⅛ yd. (⅛m) of black Chinese silk

NOTIONS : White binding for collar
Gold foil decoration
Invisible snaps (for jacket and skirt)
2" x 2" (5 x 5cm) scrap of cardboard
Decorative beads (for headdress)
⅛ yd. (⅛m) of quilt batting (for collar)

Making the Saekdong Jeogori (MULTICOLORED JACKET)

Learn each part of the Saekdong Jeogori

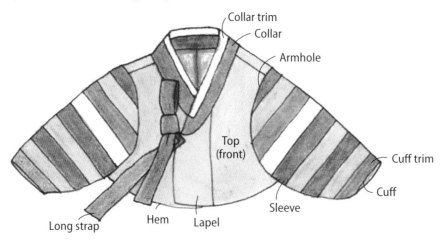

Collar trim
Collar
Armhole
Cuff trim
Cuff
Top (front)
Sleeve
Lapel
Hem
Long strap

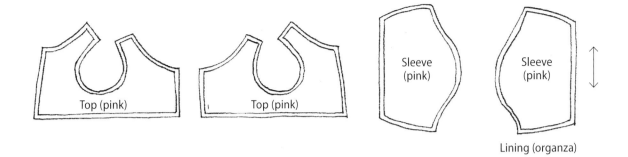

Sleeve (pink) Sleeve (pink)

Lining (organza)

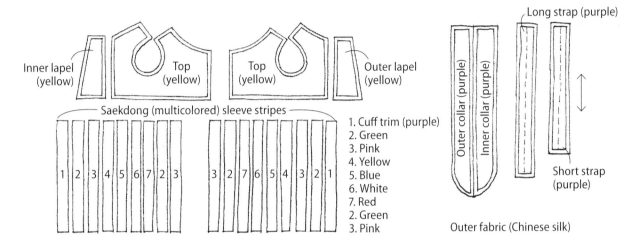

Inner lapel (yellow) Top (yellow) Top (yellow) Outer lapel (yellow)

Saekdong (multicolored) sleeve stripes

| 1 | 2 | 3 | 4 | 5 | 6 | 7 | 2 | 3 |
| 3 | 2 | 7 | 6 | 5 | 4 | 3 | 2 | 1 |

1. Cuff trim (purple)
2. Green
3. Pink
4. Yellow
5. Blue
6. White
7. Red
2. Green
3. Pink

Outer collar (purple) Inner collar (purple)

Long strap (purple)

Short strap (purple)

Outer fabric (Chinese silk)

1 **Cut the fabric pattern pieces out.** Lay the pattern pieces on the wrong side (note that to get the lapels, they must be cut off the top pattern pieces):

- **Top:** yellow silk (2)
- **Lapels:** yellow silk (2 – inner and outer)
- **Collars:** purple silk (2 – inner and outer), quilt batting (2)
- **Top (with lapel):** lining fabric (2)
- **Sleeves:** lining fabric (2)
- **Long strap** – cut a 1⅛" x 7⅞" (3 x 20cm) rectangle: purple silk (1)

- **Short strap** – cut a 1⅛" x 6" (3 x 15cm) rectangle: purple silk (1)
- **Multicolored sleeve stripes** – cut a ⅜" x 7" (1 x 18cm) rectangle: green silk (2), red silk (2), white silk (2), blue silk (2) yellow silk (2), pink silk (2)
- **Cuff trim** – cut a ⅜" x 7" (1 x 18cm) rectangle: purple silk (2)

Add a ⅜" (1cm) seam allowance around all pieces and cut them out.

Fold the seam allowance after sewing

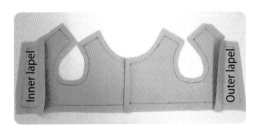

Inner lapel Outer lapel

2 **Make the outer Jeogori—stitch the back seam.** Align the edges of the center back seam with right sides together. Sew the edges together, then press the seam allowance towards the right-hand side of the garment (as if it were worn).

3 **Make the outer Jeogori—attach the lapels.** Align the inner side edges of the lapels with the side edges of the top with right sides together. Sew the edges, then press the seam allowances toward the center back seam of the garment.

4 **Make the outer Jeogori— stitch the shoulder seams.** Align the shoulder seams of the front and back of the jacket with right sides together. Sew the edge, then press the seam allowance toward the back of the garment.

5 **Make the Saekdong sleeves.** Sew all of the multicolored strips in a row following the order shown in the picture. Sew the cuff trim last, then press all the seams open. Lay the sleeve pattern over the stitched rows (one facing up, the other down), add a ⅜" (1cm) seam allowance, and cut out the patchwork. Fold under the seam allowance of the cuff trim, then fold the entire sleeve in half with right sides together and sew the side seams.

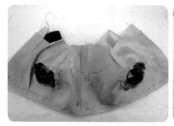

6 **Attach the sleeves.** Align the armhole edge of the sleeves with that of the top with right sides together, then sew around the perimeter of the armhole.

7 **Join the lining to the outer Jeogori.** Make the Jeogori lining the same as the outer fabric, then line it up along the raw edges of the Jeogori outer fabric. Sew them together along the center front seams and hemline, then fold under the seam allowance of the sleeve lining cuff and sew it to the outer coat cuff.

8 **Mark the collar seam.** Turn the garment right side out and iron it flat. Align the neck seam, then mark the point for the collar (according to the pattern guideline) with pins.

9 **Make the outer collar.** Layer the collar over the quilt batting and hold it in place with pins. Sew a gathering stitch 1/16" (0.1cm) outside of the seam line, then tighten the threads to have it gather around the shape of the pattern along the curved end only. Iron the fold in place.

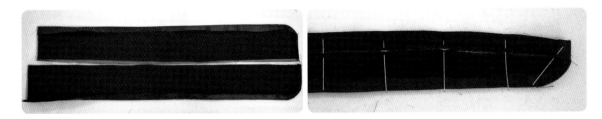

10 **Make the collar lining and join it to the outer collar.** Follow the same instructions to make the collar lining. Align the raw edge of the outer collar and lining with right sides facing, and sew them together.

11 **Attach the collar.** Pin the folded edge of the outer collar along the neck edge of the jacket, following the pattern guidelines. Baste it in place, then sew it on with a blind stitch. Fold the lining over the edge, and sew it in place with a blind stitch as well.

12 **Make the straps.** Fold the straps in half lengthwise with right sides together, then sew them along one long edge and one short edge, leaving one short edge free. Turn them right side out and iron them flat.

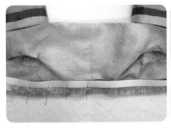

13 **Attach the straps.** Sew one end of the long strap at the point where the outer collar and outer lapel meet. Sew one end of the short strap where the pattern guidelines indicate.

14 **Attach the collar trim.** Fold under the short edges of the collar trim and press them in place. Align it to the inside of the collar, and sew it in place with a ⅜" (1cm) seam allowance. Flip the strip over to the right side and blind stitch the other long raw edge in place.

15 **Attach the invisible snaps.** Sew the prong side of the snaps to the outside of the inner lapel and the sockets to the inside of the outer lapel to finish.

Making the Chima (SKIRT)

Learn each part of the Chima

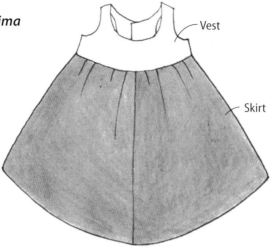

Vest

Skirt

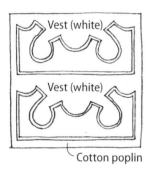

Vest (white)

Vest (white)

Cotton poplin

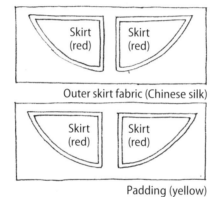

Skirt (red)　Skirt (red)

Outer skirt fabric (Chinese silk)

Skirt (red)　Skirt (red)

Padding (yellow)

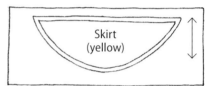

Skirt (yellow)

Lining (chiffon with peach, pomegranate and bergamot patterns)

1   **Cut the fabric pattern pieces out.** Lay the pattern pieces on the wrong side of the fabric and trace the following pattern pieces:

- **Vest:** cotton poplin (2)
- **Skirt:** Chinese silk – outer fabric (2), Korean silk – padding (2)

- **Skirt lining (with pieces joined):** Patterned chiffon (2)

Add a ⅜" (1cm) seam allowance around all edges and cut the fabric pieces out.

2   **Join the skirt pieces.**
Align the short straight edges of the outer skirt pieces together with right sides facing and sew along the edge. Press the seam allowance towards the right-hand side (as if wearing). Repeat this with the padding pieces.

Fold the seam allowances to the right after sewing.

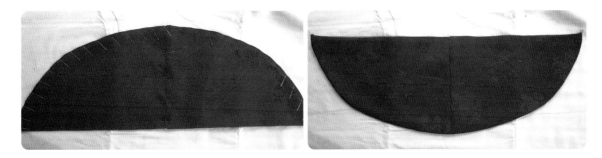

3 **Join the outer skirt and padding.** Layer the outer skirt with the skirt padding with right sides facing and sew along the curved hem. Trim the seam allowance, turn the piece right side out, and iron.

4 **Make the skirt lining.** Make a double-fold hem on the edge of the yellow skirt lining by folding up the bottom edge ¼" (0.5cm) twice. Sew the hem in place with a blind stitch.

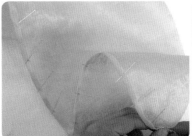
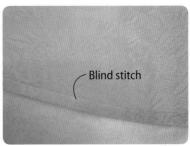

Blind stitch

5 **Join the outer skirt and lining.** Align the outer skirt and the skirt lining with right sides facing out, then sew them together along the waistline.

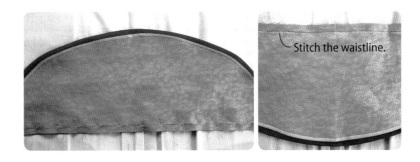

Stitch the waistline.

6 **Gather the skirt on the waistline.** Run gathering stitches along the waistline of the skirt ⅜" (1cm) from the edge. Pull at the threads to create gathers going in towards the middle of the skirt. Gather the skirt until it is as wide as the waistline of the vest section.

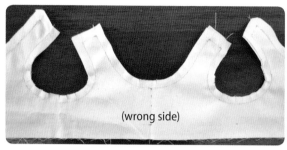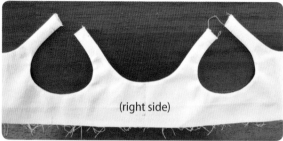

(wrong side)　　　　(right side)

7 **Make the vest.** Align the vest pieces together with right sides facing and sew along the edges, leaving the shoulder and waistline seams open. Trim the seam allowances to ¼" (0.5cm), cut notches at the armholes, turn the vest right side out, and iron it flat.

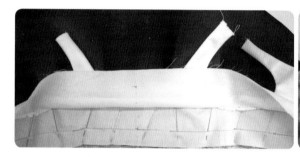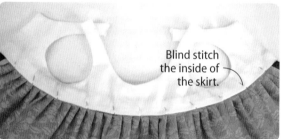

Blind stitch the inside of the skirt.

8 **Join the vest and the skirt.** Align the waistline seams of the vest and skirt with right sides facing. Pin the skirt to just the outer vest fabric, then sew the edges together. Fold under the seam allowance of the vest lining, then align it to cover the previous seam. Sew it in place with a blind stitch.

You can also fold under the seam allowances on the shoulder seam of the back vest, then tuck the raw edge of the front vest into the tube to cover up the seam allowance. You can then press and sew the layers in place directly from the front side of the vest so no seam allowances show.

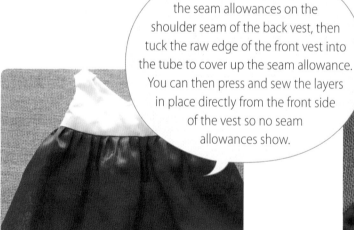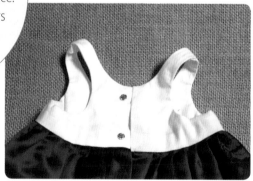

9 **Stitch the shoulder seams.** Align the shoulder seam of the front and back vest with right sides facing and sew them together. Overlock the seam allowance, then edge stitch it from the right side.

10 **Attach the invisible snaps.** Attach the invisible snaps on the vest placket.

Making the Gulle (DECORATIVE HEADDRESS)

Learn each part of the Gulle

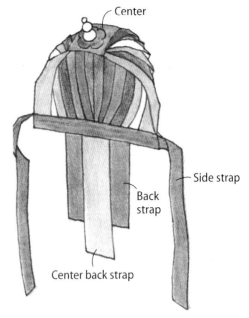

Center

Side strap

Back strap

Center back strap

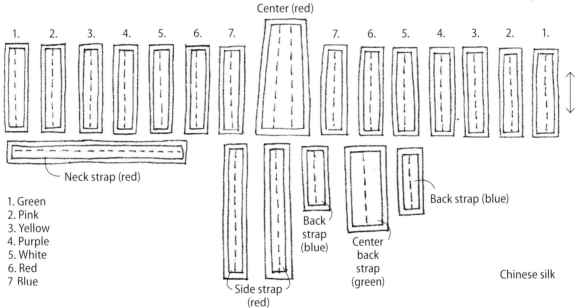

Center (red)

1. 2. 3. 4. 5. 6. 7. 7. 6. 5. 4. 3. 2. 1.

Neck strap (red)

1. Green
2. Pink
3. Yellow
4. Purple
5. White
6. Red
7 Blue

Side strap (red)

Back strap (blue)

Center back strap (green)

Back strap (blue)

Chinese silk

1 **Cut the fabric pattern pieces out.** Lay the pattern pieces on the wrong side of the fabric and trace the following pattern pieces:

- **Colored strips** – cut a 2¾" x 9" (7 x 23cm) rectangle: green silk (2), pink silk (2), yellow silk (2), purple silk (2), white silk (2), red silk (2), blue silk (2)
- **Center strap** – cut a 4⅜" x 9" (11 x 23cm) rectangle: red silk (1)
- **Neck strap** – cut a 7" x 1½" (18 x 4cm) rectangle: red silk (1)

- **Side straps** – cut a 9½" x 1⅜" (24 x 3.5cm) rectangle: red silk (2)
- **Center back strap** – cut a 3½" x 6⅜" (9 x 16cm) rectangle: green silk (1)
- **Back straps** – cut a 2¾" x 4¾" (7 x 12cm) rectangle: blue silk (2)
- **Flower decoration** – cut a 3⅛" x 3⅛" (8 x 8cm) square: black silk (1)

Cut the fabric pieces out; the seam allowance is already included.

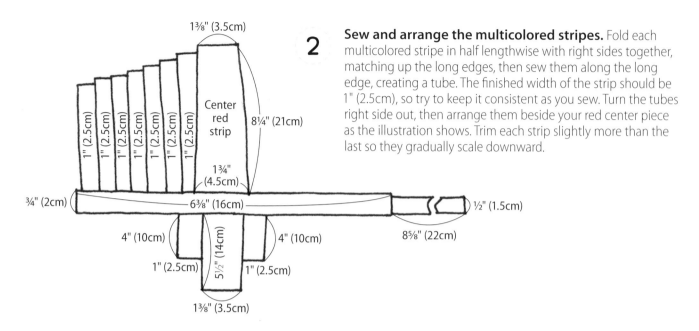

2 **Sew and arrange the multicolored stripes.** Fold each multicolored stripe in half lengthwise with right sides together, matching up the long edges, then sew them along the long edge, creating a tube. The finished width of the strip should be 1" (2.5cm), so try to keep it consistent as you sew. Turn the tubes right side out, then arrange them beside your red center piece as the illustration shows. Trim each strip slightly more than the last so they gradually scale downward.

3 **Make the center of the Gulle.** Turn the center piece in half lengthwise with right sides together, matching up the long edges. From the raw edge, mark a line ⅜" (1cm) in from the top corner down to the bottom corner; trim along that edge so your finished piece will be a trapezoid. Now stitch the edges together, turn the tube right side out, and press the piece while the seam is in the middle, as the photo shows.

4 **Make the back straps.** Fold the green and blue back straps in half lengthwise, matching up the long edges. Sew them together along the long edge and one short edge, clip the corners, turn the strips right side out, and press them.

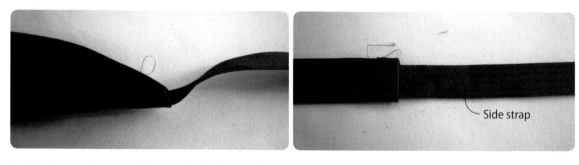

5 **Make the neck strap.** Turn under the long edges of the neck strap by ⅜" (1cm) and iron, then do the same for the short edges of the strap. Fold and iron the strap in half lengthwise with wrong sides together. Sew the two side straps similarly to the back straps, sewing them along one long and short edge. Tuck the raw end of the side strap inside the neck strap, then fold the neck strap around it. Sew the end of the strap in place across this fold.

6 **Attach the multicolored strips to the center piece.** Lay the ends of the trimmed strips along the wrong side of the center piece, about one third of the way down the top of the center piece. Fan them out as seen in the photo, so they gradually move down and rotate outward to create the fan effect. Once they've been placed as you like, baste them. Then fold under the top third of the center piece to cover the raw edges. Blind stitch this section in place from the wrong side, being sure to turn under the raw edge from the center piece as well.

7 **Join the neck strap to the multicolored strips.** Arrange the multicolored strips from the previous step along the neck strap, maintaining their fanned position. Sew them to the turned-under fold from one side of the neck strap, then fold over the other side of the neck strap to cover the seam allowance and blind stitch the edge in place.

8 **Attach the back straps.** Arrange the green center back strap and two blue back straps at the center of the red neck strap with finished ends pointing up. Sew them in place, then fold them downward and sew tiny prick stitches at the edges to tack the fold in place. See page 132 to add the gold foil pattern to the neck strap and back straps.

9 **Add the flower décor.** Cut a piece of cardboard following the flower pattern. Glue it to a piece of black fabric, then fold under the edges of the fabric to clean it up. Print the gold foil flower pattern on the fabric, and attach some jade beads for decoration. To finish, blind stitch the flower to the center of the Gulle.

"Hanbok" for First Birthdays

Hanbok (traditional Korean celebratory dress) Outfit for Boys

Includes: obangjang durumagi (overcoat), baji (pants), bokgeon (decorative pointed hat), and dolddi (belt)

SIZES | XS through L

FABRIC | **Obangjang Durumagi (Overcoat):**
¼–⅓ yd. (¼–⅓m) of yellow Chinese silk
½–⅔ yd. (½–⅔m) of green Chinese silk
⅓–½ yd. (⅓–½m) of purple Chinese silk
¼ yd. (¼m) of red Chinese silk
⅛ yd. (⅛m) of blue Chinese silk
½–⅔ yd. (½–⅔m) of organza for lining

Baji (Pants):
¼ yd. (¼m) of Chinese silk
½ yd. (½m) of cotton poplin
½ yd. (½m) of Korean silk for lining

Bokgeon (Decorative Pointed Hat):
⅓–½ yd. (⅓–½m) of black cotton poplin

FABRIC, continued | **Dolddi (Belt):**
⅛ yd. (⅛m) of yellow Chinese silk
⅛ yd. (⅛m) of green Chinese silk
⅛ yd. (⅛m) of red Chinese silk
⅛ yd. (⅛m) of blue Chinese silk
⅛ yd. (⅛m) of pink Chinese silk

NOTIONS | White collar binding
Gold decorative foil
Invisible snaps
⅛ yd. (⅛m) of quilt batting (for collar)
Batting for belt

Making Obangjang Durumagi (OVERCOAT)

Learn each part of the Durumagi

1 **Cut the fabric pattern pieces out.** Lay the patterns on the wrong side of the outer fabrics and trace the following pattern pieces:

- **Coat back:** green silk (2), lining (2)
- **Coat front:** green silk (2), lining (2)
- **Sleeve:** red silk (2), lining (2)

- **Coat side:** purple silk (2), lining (2)
- **Lapel:** yellow silk (2)
- **Front lining** (cut lapel and front as one piece): lining (2)

- **Collar:** blue silk (2)
- **Long strap** – cut a (3 x 23cm) rectangle: blue silk (1)
- **Short strap** – cut a (3 x 17cm) rectangle: blue silk (1)

Add a ⅜" (1cm) seam allowance to all the pieces, except for the seam lining cuff, which needs ⅝" (1.5cm), then cut the fabric pieces out.

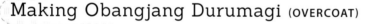

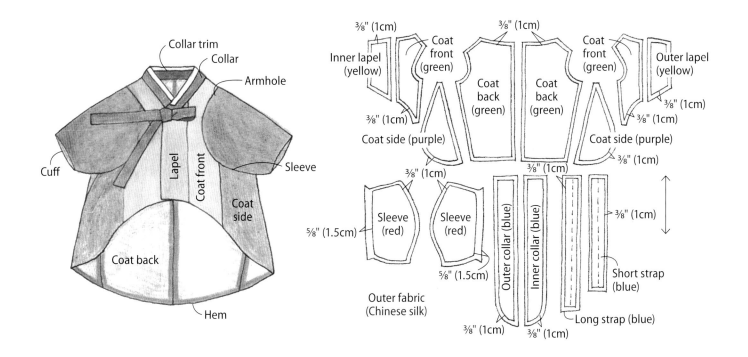

Collar trim
Collar
Armhole
Cuff
Lapel
Coat front
Sleeve
Coat side
Coat back
Hem

³⁄₈" (1cm)
Inner lapel (yellow)
Coat front (green)
Coat back (green)
Coat back (green)
Coat front (green)
³⁄₈" (1cm)
Outer lapel (yellow)
³⁄₈" (1cm)
³⁄₈" (1cm)
³⁄₈" (1cm)
Coat side (purple)
Coat side (purple)
³⁄₈" (1cm)
³⁄₈" (1cm)
Sleeve (red)
Sleeve (red)
⁵⁄₈" (1.5cm)
⁵⁄₈" (1.5cm)
³⁄₈" (1cm)
Outer collar (blue)
Inner collar (blue)
³⁄₈" (1cm)
Short strap (blue)
Long strap (blue)
Outer fabric (Chinese silk)
³⁄₈" (1cm)
³⁄₈" (1cm)

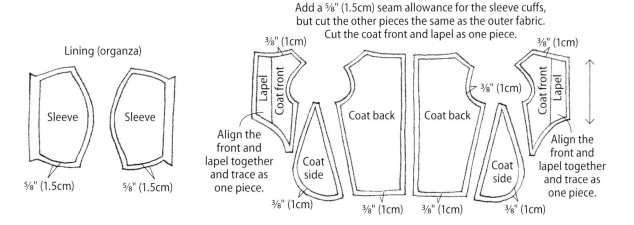

Lining (organza)

Sleeve
Sleeve
⁵⁄₈" (1.5cm)
⁵⁄₈" (1.5cm)

Add a ⁵⁄₈" (1.5cm) seam allowance for the sleeve cuffs, but cut the other pieces the same as the outer fabric. Cut the coat front and lapel as one piece.

³⁄₈" (1cm)
Lapel
Coat front
Align the front and lapel together and trace as one piece.
Coat side
Coat back
Coat back
³⁄₈" (1cm)
Coat front
Lapel
³⁄₈" (1cm)
Align the front and lapel together and trace as one piece.
Coat side
³⁄₈" (1cm)
³⁄₈" (1cm)
³⁄₈" (1cm)
³⁄₈" (1cm)

Fold in the seam allowance after sewing.

2 **Stitch the center seam of the back pieces.** Layer the coat back pieces together with right sides facing along the back seam. Sew them together along this seam, then iron the seam allowance to the right-hand side (as if wearing).

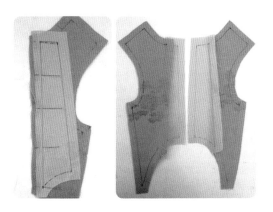

3 **Attach the lapel on the coat front.** Align the edges of the lapel and coat front pieces with right sides together. Sew them along this edge, then iron the seam allowances toward the right-hand side (as if wearing).

4 **Sew the side pieces.** Align the edges of the coat back and side pieces with right sides together. Sew them along this edge, then iron the seam allowances toward the coat back. Repeat this with the edge of the coat side and the coat front, sewing the edges together and ironing the seam allowances towards the back.

5 **Stitch the shoulder seams of the front and back sides.** Align the shoulder seams of the coat front and back with right sides together. Sew them along this edge, then iron the seam allowance towards the back.

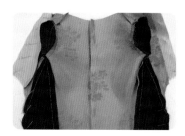

6 **Sew the sleeves and attach to the body.** Fold the sleeves in half with right sides together and sew them along the side seams. Align the armhole edge of the sleeve with that of the coat body and sew around the perimeter. Repeat steps 2–6 for the lining pieces as well to create the lining of the coat.

7 **Join the coat and lining.** Layer the coat and lining together with right sides facing and aligning the raw edges. Sew them together along the center front edge of the coat and the hemline.

8 **Join the sleeve and lining.** Match up the raw edges of the sleeves and sew them together.

9 Secure the collar position. Turn the coat right side out, then iron the seams and lining. Mark the stitching line for the collar with pins.

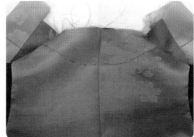 

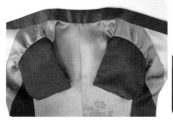 

10 **Attach the collar.** Baste the quilt batting to the outer collar ¹⁄₁₆" (0.1cm) outside the seam line. Fold in the seam allowance along the curved edge and press it flat. Repeat this with the inner collar piece as well. Sew the outer collar and lining together along the straight edge. Bind the raw edge of the coat neckline with the collar pieces, basting the folded edge of the collar onto the coat. Sew it in place with a blind stitch.

11 **Make the straps.** Fold the long and short straps in half lengthwise with right sides together and sew them along the long edge and one short edge. Turn them right side out and iron them flat. Sew the raw edge of the long strap where the collar meets the lapel along the seam line. Sew the short strap on the other half of the coat where the pattern indicates.

12 **Attach the collar trim.** Take the collar trim and fold under each short edge by ³⁄₈". Align it along the edge of the collar, then sew it in place with a ³⁄₈" (1cm) seam allowance. Press the trim away from the collar, then fold it back under to the underside of the collar and blind stitch it in place.

13 **Attach invisible snaps and print the gold foil patterns.** Attach invisible snaps to the coat and print the gold foil patterns (see page 132) on the collar.

Making the Baji (PANTS)

Learn each part of the Baji

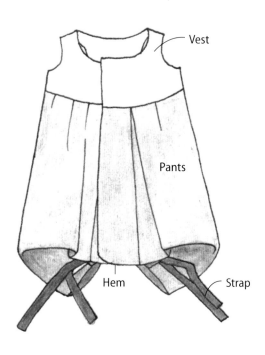

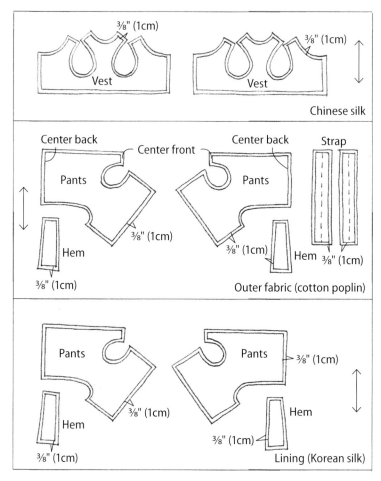

Vest — ⅜" (1cm)   ⅜" (1cm) — Vest
Vest   Vest
Chinese silk

Center back   Center front   Center back   Strap
Pants   Pants
Hem   ⅜" (1cm)   ⅜" (1cm)   Hem   ⅜" (1cm)
⅜" (1cm)
Outer fabric (cotton poplin)

Pants   Pants   ⅜" (1cm)
Hem   ⅜" (1cm)   Hem
⅜" (1cm)   ⅜" (1cm)   Lining (Korean silk)

1 **Cut the fabric pattern pieces out.** Lay the patterns on the wrong side of the outer fabrics and trace the following pattern pieces:

- **Vest:** Chinese silk (2)
- **Pants:** cotton poplin (2), lining (2)
- **Hem:** cotton poplin (2), lining (2)
- **Straps** – cut a 1⅛" x 9" (3 x 23cm) rectangle: cotton poplin (2)

Add ⅜" (1cm) seam allowances around all the pieces, then cut the fabric out.

2 **Sew the pants.** Align the center back seam of the pants to the slanted line of the hem piece with right sides facing; pin and sew the edges in place. Iron the seam allowance towards the pants.

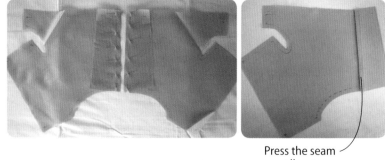

Press the seam
allowance.

3 **Stitch the center front seam.** Align the center front edges of the pants together with right sides facing and sew them together along the edge. Press the seam open, then repeat this with the lining pieces as well.

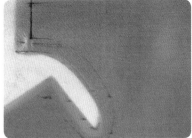

4 **Join the pants and lining, part 1.** Align the outer pants and lining pieces with right sides together and sew them along the hem and leg openings, leaving sections A and B noted in the illustration open. Cut notches at the curves of the seam allowance, then turn the pants right side out.

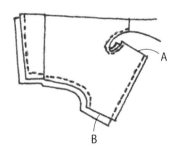
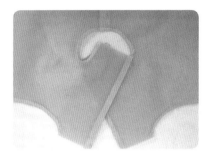

5 **Join the pants and lining, part 2.** Bring together sides A and B for one half of the pants and sew them together along this edge. Repeat for the other half of the pants, and press the seam allowance towards the back.

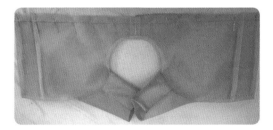

6 **Align the pants and lining edge.** Align the upper waistline edge of the pants and lining, then pin them together along the edge.

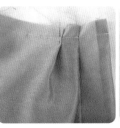

7 **Pleat the fabric on the waistline.** Pleat the fabric along the waistline going out from the center where the pattern guidelines indicate. Pin, then baste the pleats in place.

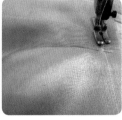

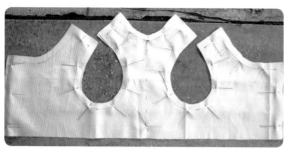

8   **Make the vest.** Layer the outer vest and lining pieces together with right sides facing and sew them together along the edges except for the shoulder and waist seams. Trim the seam allowance to ¼" (0.5cm) and cut notches in the armholes. Turn the vest right side out and iron it flat.

9   **Join the pants and the vest, part 1.** Align the waistline of the vest with that of the pants with right sides facing. Pin the pants to the outer vest fabric only, then sew the edges together.

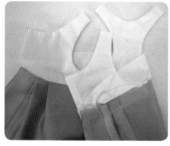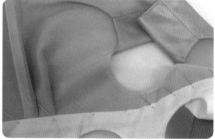

10   **Join the pants and the vest, part 2.** Fold under the seam allowance on the vest lining, then pin it in place, covering over the previous seam. Blind stitch the fold in place. Align the shoulder edges with right sides together and sew along the edges. Overlock the seam allowances and press them open. Edge stitch the finished seam.

11   **Attach the straps and snaps.** Fold under the short edges of the straps, then fold the strap in half lengthwise with right sides together. Sew it in half along the long edge, then turn the strap right side out. Sew them on the pants, then attach invisible snaps to the placket front to finish.

Making the Bokgeon (DECORATIVE FOLDED HAT)

Learn each part of the Bokgeon

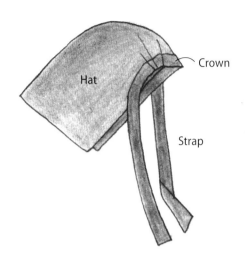

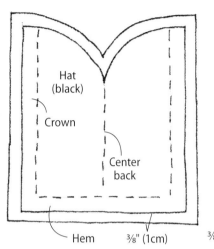

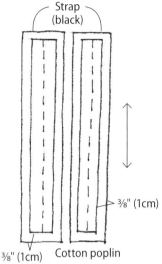

1 **Cut the fabric pattern pieces out.** Trace 1 hat and 2 strap – 11" x 1½" (28 x 4cm) rectangle – pieces on the wrong side of the fabric. Add a ⅜" (1cm) seam allowance, then cut the fabric pieces out.

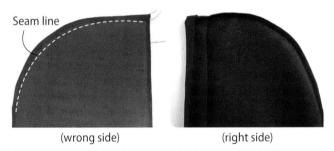

2 **Sew the top of the hat.** Fold the hat piece in half with right sides together, then sew the curved edge. Press the seam, then iron it towards the right-hand side.

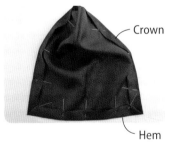

3 **Make the straps.** Sew the 2 straps (see page 117 for instructions). Then, fold under the seam allowances along the crown line and hem of the hat and blind stitch the fold in place.

4 **Make pleats.** Following the pattern guidelines, make two pleats on the crown of the hat. Slip the straps into the pleats and sew them in place.

5 **Print the gold foil for decoration.** Put the gold foil on the fabric. Set the iron temperature to silk, then press for 1 minute; don't move the iron during this time to ensure the best results. After it cools, tear off the excess gold foil. Put a thin cloth on top of the foil and iron it again to remove the luster.

Making the Dolddi (BELT)

Learn each part of the Dolddi

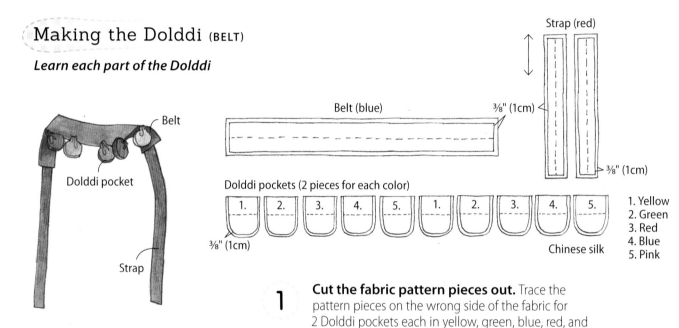

Strap (red)

Belt (blue)   ⅜" (1cm)

⅜" (1cm)

Belt

Dolddi pocket

Strap

Dolddi pockets (2 pieces for each color)

1. 2. 3. 4. 5. 1. 2. 3. 4. 5.

⅜" (1cm)   Chinese silk

1. Yellow
2. Green
3. Red
4. Blue
5. Pink

1 **Cut the fabric pattern pieces out.** Trace the pattern pieces on the wrong side of the fabric for 2 Dolddi pockets each in yellow, green, blue, red, and pink. Trace a 9⅞" x 2⅜" (25 x 6cm) rectangle for the blue belt, and two 9" x 1½" (23 x 4cm) rectangles for the red straps. Add a ⅜" (1cm) seam allowance to the pieces and cut them out.

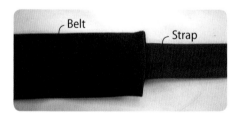

Belt   Strap

2 **Make Dolddi pockets.** Make the Dolddi pockets from the 5 colors (yellow, green, red, blue, and pink) by sewing the two layers together along the curved edge. Turn the pocket right side out, then fold it under along the pattern guideline.

3 **Make the belt.** Fold the straps in half lengthwise with right sides together, and sew them along one long edge and one short edge. Turn them right side out from the remaining short edge and press them flat. Turn under the seam allowances of the belt along all edges, then fold the belt in half lengthwise with wrong sides together. Tuck the raw edge of the straps between the short end folds of the belt, and edge stitch around the belt to anchor the straps in place.

4 **Attach Dolddi pockets to the belt.**
Print the gold foil patterns on the Dolddi pockets, belt, and straps. Fill the pockets with batting, then run a gathering stitch along the pocket openings. Cinch up the pockets, then sew them onto the belt.

Making Tarae Busun (DECORATIVE SOCKS)

SIZES	XS through L
FABRIC	⅛–¼ yd. (⅛–¼m) of white cotton poplin
NOTIONS	Red and blue embroidery floss

Learn each part of Tarae Busun

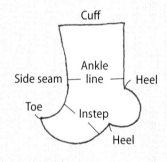

Cuff

Ankle line

Side seam

Heel

Toe

Instep

Heel

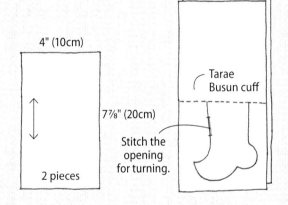

4" (10cm)

7⅞" (20cm)

2 pieces

Tarae Busun cuff

Stitch the opening for turning.

1 **Layer two pieces of fabric, then fold them in half to make a crease.** Unfold them, then align the cuff edge of the sock at the crease and trace the pattern onto the fabric. Stitch the small area for the opening.

2 **Fold the fabric back along the crease (making 4 layers) and sew along the traced seams, except for the seam sewn previously.** Back stitch several times over the heels for the best strength. Trim the seam allowances to ¼" (0.5cm) and cut notches at the heels. Hold onto the top layer and turn the fabric right side out. Poke a threaded needle through the toe to get it to pop out perfectly. You can iron the instep seam while you do this for the best shape. Sew a French knot for the tip of the toe, and sew the opening closed.

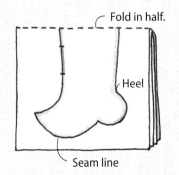

Fold in half.

Heel

Seam line

portable bag for puppies

Denim Pet Carrier

This bag is designed as a shoulder bag with a safety neck belt inside and a pocket on the back for carrying items for trips with your dog, such as tissues, snacks and doggie doo bags. There are ventilation holes designed on the front and side of the bag, which are not only useful for ventilation but also for your dog to enjoy the view.

Wow, it's so soft!

Denim Pet Carrier

FINISHED SIZE	15⅜" x 10¼" x 7⅞" (39 x 26 x 20cm) not including strap
FABRIC	1 yd. (1m) of 10oz. denim for outer bag 1 yd. (1m) of striped cotton/ linen blend for lining ¼ yd. (¼m) of mesh fabric
NOTIONS	1 yd. (1m) of fusible fleece interfacing Plastic board for bottom of bag: 14¾" x 7⅞" (37.5 x 20cm) One hook ring Five snap buttons (metal snaps or regular buttons would also work) One wooden button ½ yd. (½m) of cotton ribbon for leash strap 8⅝" (22cm) of ⅝" (1.5cm) wide leather strap One swivel hook ring Batting for cushion 4¾ yds. (4¾m) of 1½" (4cm) wide bias tape

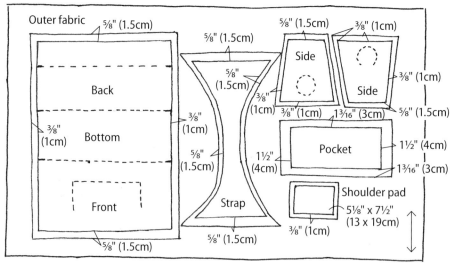

Outer fabric

⅝" (1.5cm)

Back

⅜" (1cm) Bottom

Front

⅝" (1.5cm)

⅝" (1.5cm)

⅝" (1.5cm)

⅜" (1cm)

⅝" (1.5cm)

Strap

⅝" (1.5cm)

⅝" (1.5cm)

⅜" (1cm)

⅜" (1cm)

Side

Side

⅝" (1.5cm)

⅜" (1cm)

⅜" (1cm)

⅜" (1cm)

1³⁄₁₆" (3cm)

⅝" (1.5cm)

Pocket

1½" (4cm)

1½" (4cm)

1³⁄₁₆" (3cm)

Shoulder pad
5⅛" x 7½" (13 x 19cm)

⅜" (1cm)

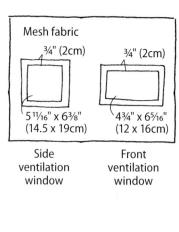

Mesh fabric

¾" (2cm)

¾" (2cm)

5¹¹⁄₁₆" x 6⅜" (14.5 x 19cm)

4¾" x 6⁵⁄₁₆" (12 x 16cm)

Side ventilation window

Front ventilation window

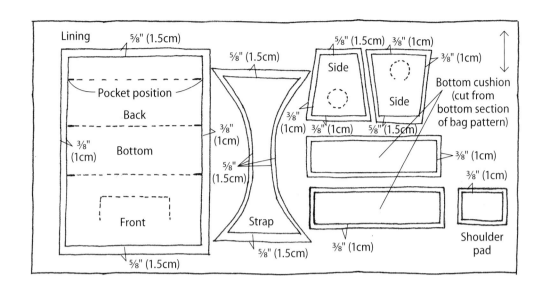

1. **Cut the fabric pattern pieces out.** Lay the pattern pieces on the wrong side of the fabric and trace the pattern. Add the necessary seam allowances as the illustrations suggest. Mark the side pocket and ventilation window (front and side) positions on the fusible fleece. Cut out the fleece pieces with no seam allowance.

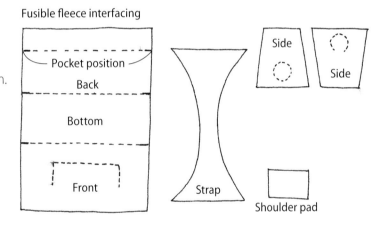

Fusible fleece interfacing

2. **Fuse the quilting to the outer fabric.** Layer the fusible fleece to the wrong side of the outer bag pieces (1 bag body, 2 sides, 1 strap, and 1 shoulder pad). Iron the fleece in place from the right side of the fabric. Cut out the ventilation window on the front and side, following the openings already cut on the fleece.

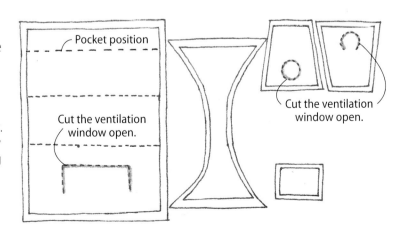

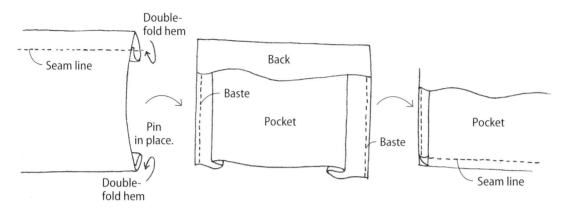

3 **Attach the pocket on the back shell piece.** Make a double-fold hem along the top edge of the pocket, then sew the hem in place. Fold the bottom edge twice and pin it in place. Layer the pocket over the back side of the bag and baste it in place along the left and right sides. Make pleats at the bottom of the pocket so that the bottom edge matches the width of the bag back. When the pleats are to your liking, edge stitch the bottom edge in place.

4 **Join the body and side outer pieces.** Join the bottom edges of the bag sides between the markings indicated on the pattern. Sew over the seam several times for the strongest finish. Next, fold the back and front of the bag upward to meet the side edges and sew them in place. Cut notches at the corners, then turn the bag right side out.

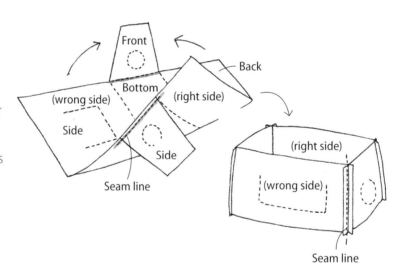

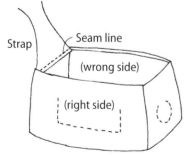

5 **Attach the outer strap.** Sew the outer bag side and strap pieces together along the top edge. If your dog is heavier, remember to stitch over the seam several times for a strong finish. Repeat steps 4 and 5 with the lining pieces, then turn the lining wrong side out.

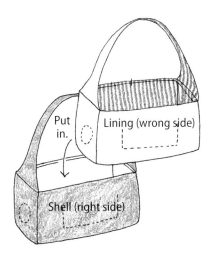

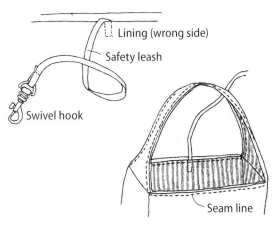

6 **Join the outer bag and lining, part 1.** Put the lining into the outer bag with wrong sides facing.

7 **Join the outer bag and lining, part 2.** Decide on where you would like to position the cotton ribbon for the safety leash, then pin it in place. Install the swivel hook on the other side of the strap. Fold in the seam allowances of the outer bag and lining, press the folds, and sew them together.

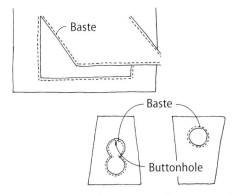

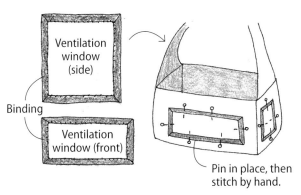

8 **Bind the ventilation windows.** In order to keep the outer fabric and lining from separating, you need to bind the edges of the ventilation windows. Baste along the edges of the front and side ventilation windows, then bind with bias tape. Also bind the edge of the round windows. When finished, sew a buttonhole on the ventilation window cover.

9 **Make the ventilation windows.** Fold under the four edges of the mesh fabric pieces and sew them in place. After sewing, bind the edges with bias tape. Turn the bag body wrong side out, pin the mesh fabric in place from the right side of the bag lining, and sew them in place. After sewing, turn the bag right side out.

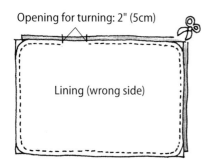

Opening for turning: 2" (5cm)

Lining (wrong side)

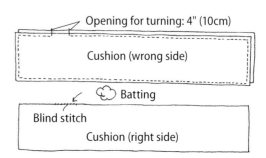

Opening for turning: 4" (10cm)

Cushion (wrong side)

Batting

Blind stitch

Cushion (right side)

10 **Make the shoulder pad.** Trim the fabric to round the four corners of the shoulder pad outer fabric and lining pieces, then align them together with right sides facing and sew them around the edges, leaving a 2" (5cm) opening for turning. Turn the shoulder pad right side out, then edge stitch the previous seams. Install the snaps at the four corners, with the prong sides along one long edge and the socket sides along the other.

12 **Finish.** Lift up the front ventilation cover and attach two snap buttons on the corners. Also attach snaps to the center of the back pocket. Attach the wooden button on top of the side ventilation window, using the buttonhole to button it up. Cut the leather strap to a length that is proportional to your dog, then attach one end with a ring snap at the back of the bag and the other end with a snap button at the front. If you don't have a ring snap, you can sew it in place instead. Cut the bottom board to the desired size and install it in the bottom of the bag with the cushion on top. Finally, snap the shoulder pad around the strap.

11 **Make the cushion.** Layer the two cushion fabric pieces together with right sides facing and sew around the perimeter, leaving a small opening for turning. Turn the cushion right side out, fill it with batting through the opening, then close it up with blind stitches.

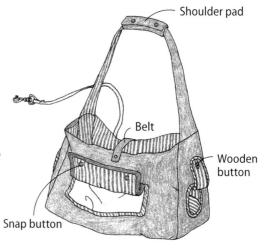

Shoulder pad

Belt

Wooden button

Snap button

Dog Clothing Tips

What do I need to know when dressing up my dog?

Humans wear clothing to keep warm and to protect their skin. Dogs, however, have hair for those purposes already. Therefore, it is better to put clothes on dogs only when going outside or when it is getting cold. For shaggy dogs, you can comb their hair after taking off the clothing to prevent the their hair getting tangled. If you find your dog has any sort of skin inflammation, you should wait until his skin condition is stable to put clothes on him again.

It is not recommended to put shoes on dogs. It might seem like putting shoes on dogs isn't a problem, but it is similar to putting high heels on humans: although we can walk, it is not comfortable at all.

If you want to tie your dog's hair or tie accessories on their ears and tails, you need to make sure there is nothing abnormal on their skin first. Be careful not to tie things on too tightly—that could cause hair loss.

When putting clothing on their dog for the first time, many owners force their dog's head and four limbs through the holes even when the clothing is too small. Forcing dogs to wear clothes, especially too-small clothes, will not only result in their extreme reluctance to wear clothes in the future, but will also cause too much pressure on their bodies. Even more seriously, it could cause joint discomfort.

After putting clothes on dogs, be sure to check if there are any problems, such as if their arms, legs, armpits, and neck are fitted too tightly, whether they can move freely, and whether there is static electricity shocking them.

How do I take care of my dog's clothing and accessories?

Use the proper detergent for the fabric the clothing is made from, and hand wash instead of machine washing. After washing, wring the clothing gently, dry them in the sun, and then iron them. By following this procedure, you can ensure that the clothing keeps its original shape. If your dog has sensitive skin, you can use a special detergent for babies.

Dog cushions and beds must be cleaned very carefully. Without proper cleaning and maintenance, they could negatively affect your dog's health. Therefore, it is very important to take the time to clean them properly. You can use a vacuum cleaner to clean up the hairs on cushions or beds every day. You should always be sure to vacuum up any hair before washing pet bedding. After washing, hang the pieces in the shade to dry in the open air. Adjust the shape of bedding while hanging it. By following this procedure, you can lengthen the lifetime of pet bedding.

Index

More Fun Things to Sew for Your Dog

If you love the adorable dog clothing featured in *Making Clothes for Your Dog*, you'll be thrilled to hear there's more to come! Tingk's next book from Design Originals will offer a wide array of doggie accessories for you to make for your pooch. You will learn to create soft toys, cute collars and neckties, baskets for storage, cushions for relaxing, several handy bags to accompany you on your canine adventures, delightful hats to ward off the sun, and more!

ISBN 978-1-57421-862-6 $19.99
DO5436
Look for Tingk's upcoming sequel at your local bookstore or specialty retailer, or at d-originals.com

More Great Books from Design Originals

**Handmade Leather
Bags & Accessories**
ISBN 978-1-57421-716-2 **$19.99**
DO5036

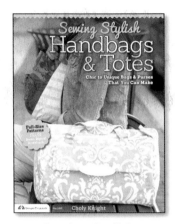

**Sewing Stylish
Handbags & Totes**
ISBN 978-1-57421-422-2 **$22.99**
DO5393

Sew Me! Sewing Basics
ISBN 978-1-57421-423-9 **$19.99**
DO5394

Sew Me! Sewing Home Decor
ISBN 978-1-57421-504-5 **$14.99**
DO5425

Parachute Cord Craft
ISBN 978-1-57421-371-3 **$9.99**
DO3495

Sewing Leather Accessories
ISBN 978-1-57421-623-3 **$14.99**
DO5313

Sewing Pretty Little Things
ISBN 978-1-57421-611-0 **$19.99**
DO5301

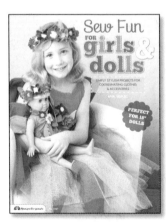

Sew Fun for Girls & Dolls
ISBN 978-1-57421-364-5 **$11.99**
DO3487

Seaside Quilts
ISBN 978-1-57421-431-4 **$24.99**
DO5402

Look for These Books at Your Local Bookstore or Specialty Retailer or at *www.D-Originals.com*